# CRISIS OF BELIEF

SERMONS FOR TODAY

# CRISIS OF BELIEF

## Murdo Ewen Macdonald

LONDON
EPWORTH PRESS

SBN 7162 0198 4

Printed in Great Britain
at the St Ann's Press, Park Road, Altrincham

# CONTENTS

# 1) The Search for Meaning

*'Thou tellest my wanderings : Put thou my tears
into thy bottle.'* Psalm 56:8

DR. VICTOR FRANKL, psychiatrist and author, spent
a number of years in Auschwitz concentration camp.
His father and mother, his wife and brother were sent
to the gas ovens. Deprived of every earthly possession,
subjected to inhuman brutality, suffering from hunger
and cold, hourly expecting extermination, he not only
survived but he succeeded in building a world-famous
school of psycho-therapy in Vienna. His whole message
can be summed up in the words 'There is no healing
without meaning'.

It was a desperate situation. His graphic description
of the way he entered Auschwitz needs no embellishing.
Fifteen hundred prisoners were told to leave their
luggage in the train and to fall into two lines. They were
made to file past a senior SS officer. He was a tall man
in spotless uniform. Standing by the gate leading into
the camp, he had assumed an attitude of careless ease.
His right hand was lifted, and with the forefinger he
pointed leisurely to the right and to the left. At the
time none of the dishevelled band of prisoners had the
slightest idea of the sinister meaning behind the movement of the officer's finger, pointing now to the right
and now to the left, but far more frequently to the left.

The significance of the forefinger game was explained

1

to Victor Frankl that very evening. Ninety per cent were sent to the left. Like cattle they were driven to a building which had the word 'bath' written over its doors in several European languages. On entering each prisoner was given a bar of soap. If you were to ask one of the prisoners who moved right what happened to those who moved left, he would point to a tall chimney belching out a column of flame and smoke into the grey sky of Poland. That's what happened to the ninety per cent and it all depended on the movement of one man's forefinger. It was in such a place that Victor Frankl discovered the meaning of life.

While it would be wrong to argue that Auschwitz camp is a microcosm of the whole of life, it would be true to say that capriciousness and cruelty seem to belong to the very texture of human existence. A bird's eye view of history does not present our species in a very favourable light. Wholesale butcheries, cities sacked, libraries burned, priceless architecture destroyed are among its commonplace occurrences. Nor has Christianity itself presented a picture of charity in a fierce and warring world. Its record has been one of jarring sects, bitter controversies and bloody persecutions. Nature in conspiracy with man has been responsible for a great deal of misery. When we think of

*Blight and famine, plague and earthquakes, roaring*
*deeps and fiery sands,*
*Clanging fights and flaming towns, and sinking ships*
*and praying hands*

meaninglessness would appear to belong to what we mean by history.

It is therefore not surprising to find a number of the creative modern writers arguing that existence is meaningless, that the best we can do in the circumstances is to work out a philosophy of the absurd. So we find Sartre saying that the life of the solitary drunkard and that of the great statesmen are equally pointless. Camus seems to echo this sentiment when he says he would rather live in an absurd and indifferent cosmos in which men suffer and die meaninglessly than see every human happening encased within a pitiless framework of meaning. What they are both saying is that there is no ultimate meaning to our existence. They call on all men to create their own private meanings and purposes in the full knowledge that there is nothing inherent in the universe that will support them.

This is brave talk but does it amount to anything more than whistling in the dark? Is it possible to accept this terrifying void of meaninglessness and at the same time lead purposeful creative lives? Both Sartre and Camus seem to have succeeded but neither they themselves nor the nihilistic characters that people their books are likely to enhance or encourage those who like Tolstoy before his conversion are seriously considering suicide. Whatever the creative modern writers say man cannot create his own meaning. He may land on the moon, probe the atmosphere round Venus and build computers bordering on omniscience, but he cannot create meaning any more than he can create security.

This void of meaninglessness expresses itself in a number of ways. It sometimes takes the shape of apathy, of violence among the dispossessed, of demonic efforts on the part of the privileged to protect their own little meanings against the yawning abyss. The affluent upper middle classes have their own answers in face of the void. Alcohol, skipping from bed to bed, drugs and the pursuit of anything exciting are used as compensatory distractions. But among professional and business groups perhaps the commonest answer to meaninglessness is success. For success means significance, and a sense of our own importance assuages, for the time being, the desolating sense of emptiness within.

Man needs more than physical or material security. He needs meaning if he is to live actively and creatively. He must know that what he does, the life he leads, the activities that make up his days, will have some value in the future, for himself, for others and for the course of history. Without this sense of worthwhileness, an abyss of emptiness yawns under us, and enervation comes over us. Without this sense of meaning, grasping us from beyond ourselves, we dry up, the engine stutters and stops and we begin to die inwardly. Meaning and its close companion hope provide the fuel that stoke our aspirations and enthusiasms.

In Auschwitz camp Victor Frankl, the prisoner whose chances of survival were twenty to one against, nevertheless emerged into the larger world outside with a sense of meaning on which he reared a liberating and healing philosophy of life. Is it possible for use to do the same? It is of course only too painfully true that human existence is marked by a pathological disorder, but while this is so we must guard against the temptation to dismiss life as a tale told by an idiot. Even those who protest most loudly, Kafka, Sartre, Camus and Beckett, are under an unremitting pressure to make sense out of existence. Nor need we be ashamed of such a demand. The quest for meaning is universal, it is indeed part of existence itself. It is difficult to live without hoping that some apocalypse of meaning will finally vindicate our struggles and our strivings, even if it is winning the football pools. The most important part of the quest for meaning is the demand for endorsement of ourselves as persons, the desire to be valued for our own sakes and not merely for what we happen to achieve. We want to count.

In wrestling with the enigma of meaninglessness we must on no account forget that the central symbol of Christianity is a cross. What happened on Calvary seems to be every bit as senseless and inhuman as the exterminations in Auschwitz, yet the men who witnessed the gruesome spectacle did not become apostles of the absurd. Discerning a purpose behind all that seemed to deny sense and sanity, they too, even more passionately that Victor Frankl, proclaimed a gospel of healing, and of a deathless hope. They did not shut their eyes to the dark side of life. They talked of the whole creation, groaning in travail, but they also declared that all things worked together for good to those who believed in God. Has the Christian faith any answer to the questions that sap our energies and rob us of every semblance of meaning in this life?

Consider the problem of suffering to begin with.

And by suffering I mean not the petty privations and frustrations it is not possible to escape but what Keats calls 'The giant agony of the world'. Suffering in this sense must include not only diseases like cancer and epilepsy, not only the stunning sledgehammer blows of bereavement and premature death, not only the anguish of sensitive souls, but also phenomena like tidal waves, earthquakes and all the violent, vicious destructiveness of physical nature. In addition there is the suffering which history only imperfectly records. Think of the countless millions of people that have lived on this planet in the most terrifying of conditions. The total sum of pain, fear and dread suffered, numbs the imagination.

The person who faces up to the enigma of suffering in nature and in history needs not a skyblue faith, but one which will navigate him round all the stormy Cape Horns of the world. The senseless cruelties and calamities of this life, call not for trite philosophies and chirpy platitudes but for a faith as stark as the cross on which Jesus died in the last extremity of agony.

Towards the end of the last war a V1 bomb registered a direct hit on the headquarters of the English Presbyterian Church. The entire staff were killed. Not very far away was the headquarters of a gang of thieves, pimps and racketeers. They came through the blitz unscathed. This is the baffling thing about suffering— its cruel randomness, its appalling indifference to human merit—the indiscriminate manner in which it aims its blows without rhyme or reason.

Consider also the problem of sacrifice.

During the last war the British dropped a certain Major Seagrim behind the Japanese lines in Burma. His mission was to disrupt the enemy lines of communication and to foster rebellion among the Karens. He was brilliantly successful. So much so that the Japanese offered a big reward for his capture. The Karens though a poor people were not tempted. Baulked, the Japanese then resorted to a savage strategy. They broadcast a message which they knew Major Seagrim would pick up on his radio. It announced that unless he gave himself up within forty-eight hours, they would exterminate an entire village well known to him, men, women and children. When Seagrim received the message he went away to a sequestered spot and wrestled all night with this agonizing decision. What was the right thing to do, to do his duty as a soldier and perchance survive the war? Or surrender in order to save the lives of innocent people? In the morning he gave himself up and the Japanese beheaded him in the afternoon.

Was this act of sacrifice—we could cite a myriad number of other examples—pointless, blind folly in a heartless universe that cares not a scrap for our hopes and fears? Is this true not only of our individual heroisms, but also of the most glittering achievements of civilization? Are they too the result of self-deception destined in the end to oblivion and nothingness?

> *My name is Ozymandias, King of kings*
> *Look on my works, ye mighty and despair*
> *Nothing beside remains, Round the decay*
> *Of that colossal wreck, boundless and bare*
> *The lone and level sands stretch far away*

Consider finally the problem of death.

'Man is the product of causes', asserts Bertrand Russell, 'which had no prevision of the end they were achieving, his origin, his growth, his hopes and fears, his loves and beliefs are but the outcome of accidental collocation of atoms.' With equal eloquence Russell dismisses the belief in immortality as a piece of pious but utterly pointless wishful thinking. The physical brain does not survive death. Therefore he concluded there can be no memory, no self consciousness, not the faintest possibility of survival.

There are even thinkers who call themselves Christian who claim that Christianity has no need of this supporting pillar and rests upon far more solid foundations. How long would Christianity survive the extinction of this belief? Not long. Without it Christianity becomes no more than humanitarianism which Dostoevsky held to be the deadliest form of atheism. If men have been born for no other end that to suffer, to sacrifice and to die what is the point? There is no cause for jubilation, no valid reason for 'Hosannahs in the highest'. If that is all there is to it we can only shout amen to Somerset Maugham's creed : There is no reason for life and life has no meaning'.

Let me briefly expound the Christian doctrine of providence. It is not a groundless optimism such as is sponsored by many humanists and some Death of God theologians. Nor is it an infantile belief that God has constructed the universe to suit our own selfish ambitions and fond illusions. The Biblical doctrine of providence is mature and realistic. It does not shut its eyes to evil, human cruelty or unmerited suffering. Aware of the baffling contradictions of history, it proclaims a God who meets us in justice and in mercy. The belief in providence implies meaning. It asserts a direction in events; a direction which we sometimes experience as judgement and at other times as 'grace'.

The Christian doctrine of reward does not promise us 'pie in the sky by and by'. What it really affirms is the victorious purpose of God. It assures us that our tears and travail, our loyalties, our love and devotion are not wasted. There isn't a big hole at the heart of the universe through which they pour out and are lost. There is a meaningful order which confirms and endorses all our courageous endeavours for good. The sort of life that Jesus lived will not be nullified by absurdity. It is vindicated in his resurrection which a modern theologian calls 'The rectifying future of God'.

The ancient psalmist who wrote the words of my text had never heard of the doctrine of 'the conservation of values' as expounded by certain philosophers and theologians, but many centuries before they ever appeared he had grasped its meaning and how felicitously he expressed it—'Thou tellest my wanderings: Put thou my tears into thy bottle'. He had arrived at this conviction not from speculation but from his experience of life in both its transfiguring and terrifying aspects. With a piercing spiritual awareness the psalmist had grasped the essential meaning of the Biblical doctrine of providence. God is the preserver of all that is pure and beautiful and of good report. In the end view infinitesimal glimpses of reality, our imperfect insights and our fragmentary meanings will break through every barrier of ambiguity and absurdity and find fulfilment.

'On the earth the broken arcs, in the heaven a perfect round.'

# 2) Dynamics of Faith

*'The just shall live by Faith.'*
Romans 1:17

EVERY major work of literature is preoccupied with
the theme of 'guilt'. This was certainly so in ancient
Greece. Orestus sinned and was driven by the 'Furies'
across the earth. He found no peace till a jury of his
fellow countrymen voted forgiveness in Athens. It
was the same in Elizabethan England. Whether
Shakespeare was a Christian or not may still be an
open question, but his plays make one thing clear, he
believed in the reality of guilt. The hell Othello suffered
after strangling Desdemona, Lady Macbeth's insomnia
following the murder of King Duncan, the underlying
presuppositions, making sense of Hamlet's agony point
us to a stubborn, indissoluble fact—guilt is a fact, not
a figment of a fevered imagination. Or turn to Russia—
a country with a very different culture from sixteenth-
century England. Read Dostoevsky's classical novel,
*Crime and Punishment*, or Tolstoy's tragedy, *Anna
Karenina*, and again 'guilt' is the main theme. Nor is
America an exception. Isn't 'guilt' the theme that throbs
through Hawthorne's *Scarlet Letter*?

But what precisely is the phenomenon we call guilt?
The difficulty is that the word calls up different fields
of association for different people. To the lawyer guilt
means the infringement of a law upheld by society. To

10

the moralist guilt means the disobeying of an ethical principle. To the psychologist guilt may mean all that and something else. In his *Dictionary of Psychology* Drever defines guilt in these terms, 'Sense of wrong-doing, as an emotional attitude, generally involving emotional conflict, arising out of a real or imagined contravention of moral or social standards, in act or thought'. To the theologian guilt stems not from the infringement of an established law, or from the disobeying of an ethical principle. Thus guilt is associated with the disruption of a personal relationship between creature and creator. In the words of the Psalmist 'Against Thee, Thee only, have I sinned and done this evil in Thy sight'.

Speaking generally, the sense of guilt which stems from a consciousness of wrong doing, at times coupled with a sense of profound regret, is the province of the theologian. On the other hand, a sense of guilt, which in its genesis is unconscious or only partly unconscious; which is compulsive and obsessive, is, more correctly speaking, the province of the psychologist.

Freud accused Christianity of increasing and intensifying man's sense of guilt. This may account at least for his hostility to religion. To this must be added the fact that he was brought up an agnostic Jew in Vienna where Jews suffered persecution at the hands of Christians. Jung would also claim that Christianity has immeasurably intensified man's sense of guilt, but the explanation he advances is very different from Freud's. According to Jung, Jesus had so sensitized the conscience of mankind, that he made the whole of posterity more conscious of evil and its consequences. Oscar Pfister, another well-known psychologist, argued that though Christianity has a strong doctrine of sin, its even stronger emphasis on a loving God and the forgiveness of sins has agonized the agonizing inner torment we call guilt.

Let me briefly expound two modern views which offer a scientific explanation of the phenomenon of guilt. There is the view which argues that all mental and emotional disturbances, at least in their more serious forms, have a chemical or metabolic basis. While we must retain a measure of open-mindedness to the dislocating effects of chemical imbalance on the psyche, it is interesting to note that there are modern psychologists who are thoroughly sceptical of this theory. Would it not be wonderful if all the world's madness, stupidity and meanness could be eliminated by the use of drugs, intravenously injected or orally swallowed? While the biochemical approach has been heralded with trumpets over the last few decades, there is little empirical evidence to support the extravagant claims made on its behalf.

The other view is the celebrated one advanced by Freud. According to it guilt is essentially a neurosis. Or, as it has been expressed in popular form, there isn't such a thing as guilt, only guilt feelings. Before we damn Freud's theory as utterly worthless, we have to admit that there are expressions of religious and moral scrupulosity which are decidedly neurotic. Recently an American minister wrote a very good Ph.D. thesis on the subject of 'Ecclesiogenic Neurosis', i.e. neurosis which is specifically related to religious belief. Beyond any doubt he proved that from the Pharisees on, preoccupied as they were with straining at gnats and swallowing camels, countless numbers have been depressed by neurotic guilt, the sex-scared Apostolic Fathers, the mediaeval ascetics cruelly mortifying the flesh, the narrow world-denying sects. The Reformers did something to liberate men and women from this form of bondage, but right on the heels of the Reformation various forms of Protestant neurosis began to obtrude.

For example, let us in passing examine the contradictions inherent in Protestant Puritanism within the English-speaking world. In my native Hebrides the devout church member is not supposed to go to the cinema or to participate in sport. He is even deprived of playing the bagpipes. But he can smoke as much as he likes and he can drink whisky, wine or beer within moderate limits. I found it rather interesting that in some parts of America the very opposite is the case. A church member is applauded for participation in music and sport. These activities are counted to him for righteousness, but his particular denomination frowns on smoking and a glass of sherry, sweet or dry, is anathema.

It is important to distinguish between neurotic pathological guilt and healthy guilt. This can be seen if we take the analogy of a pathological sense of fear, and a normal healthy sense of fear. If someone were to force me into the ring with Cassius Clay and if I were to see him crowding me into a corner shouting, 'I am the greatest', I believe I would experience a healthy normal upsurge of fear. No one could accuse me of pathological anxiety—not even Freud. But, if every night before I went to sleep, I crawled under the bed to see if there were any snakes lurking there, my anxiety could be described as pathological. So if in a crisis I

13

play the coward at the expense of others like Lord Jim in Conrad's famous novel, I experience a healthy sense of guilt; indeed I would be a callous inhuman brute if I didn't. But if I indulge in an obsessional washing of my hands, trying to convince myself like Lady Macbeth in the play that this will wash away the stains on my character, real or imaginary, this is pathological. Our concern here is Paul's attitude to a normal not a pathological sense of guilt. And the answer Paul gives to guilt, man's perennial dilemma, the theme of the world's greatest literature, is summed up in one word—Justification.

The doctrine of justification by faith as Paul expounds it is a truly revolutionary one. Emil Brunner, the Swiss theologian, calls Justification 'the central miracle of the Christian faith'. No doubt there are resemblances between Paul's doctrine of justification by faith and the Jewish doctrine, but the difference is momentous and decisive. Devout Jews could only peer into a dim and uncertain future, hoping against hope that God would pronounce a favourable verdict at the last. But for Paul it was altogether different. For him and for all who had faith in Christ the liberating sentence had already been pronounced. Judaism struggled, Paul exulted. He did not pine after a problematical status, he already possessed it. His sins were annulled and justification and forgiveness went hand in hand. The altered relationship had conferred on him a new status. He was no longer an alien, he was a member of the household of God.

Justification, properly understoood, brands for ever our little prim moralisms as dirty lies. Pharisaism, ancient and modern, may boast of its devotion, its purity, its self-conscious humanitarianism, but when justification—the most revolutionary of all religious doctrines—drives its message home boasting is excluded. Our merits and accomplishments are but dust and ashes. The new relationship—the new status—is a gift; it is the product of sheer unmerited grace.

> *Just as I am, and waiting not*
> *To rid my soul of one dark blot.*

That is the meaning of acceptance. It is justification.

That justification is one of the great liberating revolutionary doctrines can be seen from a cursory glance at Church history. Justification is not a dusty controversy couched in legalistic terminology, confined to the first century. Fifteen hundred years later this doctrine delivered Luther from manic depression and possibly from suicide, and because he grasped the radical far-reaching implications he changed the course of history.

Martin Luther was a very pious monk. He ran the whole gamut of the Roman Catholic penitential system. He was impeccable in the exercise of every discipline. He mortified the flesh, wore an iron chain round his waist, fasted and prayed, and slept without blankets on the stone floor of his cell. Under the direction of Staupitz he even tried mysticism, but the chasm between his sense of his own unworthiness and God's transcendant holiness only yawned wider, and black suicidal depression robbed him of his manhoood. It was while he was reading in the tower study in the Augustinian monastery at Wittenberg that his eye lighted on the verse we find in Romans 1:17: 'The just shall live by faith.' It leapt out at him with the stunning force of a new revelation. He saw it as if he had read it for the first time. These are Luther's own words:

*Night and day I pondered until I saw the connection between the Justice of God and the statement, 'The just shall live by faith'. Then I grasped that the justice of God is that righteousness by which through grace and sheer mercy God justifies us through faith. Thereupon I felt myself to be reborn and to have gone through open doors into paradise.*

In a flash Luther saw that he could never impress God by his self-discipline, nor could he ever work his own passage to heaven. His one need was a new relationship with God and the key to that relationship was not anything he could do, but faith in something which God had already accomplished—in short, faith in Jesus Christ. Out of that experience in the reading room of the Wittenberg monastery came the dramatic break with Roman Catholicism, the birth of the Protestant Church and the democratic way of life of which you and I are the proud heirs.

Two centuries later an Oxford Don, by the name of Wesley, was worried about the state of the nation—its espousal of slavery, of economic exploitation—the practice of gambling, drunkenness and prostitution. Sincere and dedicated, he became a parish priest and later a missionary to the Indians in Georgia. In both spheres he failed miserably. He felt cold, frustrated and useless. On the evening of 24 May, 1738, Wesley attended a meeting at a little Moravian Chapel at Aldersgate Street in London. He listened to a reading of Luther's preface to Paul's Epistle to the Romans.

What then happened is best described by Wesley himself.

*About a quarter before nine, while he was describing the change which God works in the heart through faith in Christ, I felt my heart strangely warmed. I felt I did trust in Christ, Christ alone for my salvation. And an assurance was given me that he had taken away my sins, even mine, and saved me from the law of sin and death.*

Another two hundred years passed and again we find that Paul, speaking through his Epistle to the Romans, has power to revitalize and renew the Christian Church. Karl Barth is universally acclaimed the greatest theologian of the twentieth century. There are those who have called him the greatest theologian since Thomas Aquinas. And how did Barth leap into fame? By writing an explosive world-shaking book entitled *A Commentary on Paul's Epistle to the Romans*. And what is Barth's message in his commentary? Man's supreme sin is Titanism, his swaggering self-sufficiency and his inability to put himself right by his own efforts. Modern man is as dependent on *'sola gratia'*, grace alone, as Paul was, as Luther was, as John Wesley was in the Moravian meeting.

But wait! Does this doctrine make any sense to contemporary man? 'Justification by faith'—the very words have a forensic flavour, rather repellent to the modern ear. There are certain theological words which once spoke with meaning and with power and which have now become devalued. They no longer ring a bell in the modern consciousness. 'Justification by faith' seems to be a classic example. But surely the important thing is not the word or the term but the reality which lies behind them. And the Reality Paul and Luther and Wesley witness to has not changed. Man is still unable to put himself right and healing is of God.

The late Professor Paul Tillich deals with the doctrine of justification by faith in his books on theology and in his sermons. He argues that Psychoanalysis and Depth Psychology as they are practised today can teach us much in our understanding of the meaning of justification. The Depth Psychologist cannot save. He asks the right questions, he probes and lays bare the human predicament, as do the creative existentialist writers like Dostoevsky and Camus, but salvation must come from somewhere else. The Depth Psychologist can be an instrument of healing, as every friend, every child, can be an instrument of healing. But as analyst and psychologist he cannot bring healing by means of his medical methods. What is needed is the healing of the centre of personality, and this requires faith.

But Depth Psychology, while it cannot heal by itself, has taught us a great deal about the meaning of Grace. In the past, ministers of religion and devout church members were apt to confuse the Christian faith with a prim and priggish moralism. They disapproved of the drunkard, the lecher, the sexual deviant, and in no uncertain manner they communicated their disapproval. The Depth Psychologist, on the other hand, has traffic with those who are not good in the conventional moral sense. He is not shocked by the confessions of the lost. He takes them as they are. He accepts the unacceptable. He does not say to the patient 'You are a pretty disgusting type, but I accept you', but in dealing with him in patience and understanding he is in a most unmistakable manner communicating the fact that he accepts him. That, says Tillich, is the way God deals with us. He accepts the unacceptable. This is the message Christ preached in his parables, and what eventually got him into trouble when he demonstrated the meaning of Justification in practice.

This, too, is what every minister and every professing Christian should demonstrate in their dealing with other people. They must be prepared at all times to accept the unacceptable. Professor H. R. MacIntosh of Edinburgh used to say that any theology which is not rooted in human experience is suspect and almost certainly false. So in the last resort we learn the meaning of the doctrine of Justification by Faith not from our study of Paul or Luther or Barth, but from what we learn existentially in dealing with other people.

We are justified by the Grace of God and by nothing else. Grace comes from the Greek work 'Xapis' and its meaning is universally misunderstood. It has been looked upon as an extra special endowment conferred upon a man at ordination. This is the myth which lies behind sacramentalism. Others regard Grace as a sort of spiritual fluid injected into our infected souls like some divine penicillin. But this is nonsense. The word 'Xapis' means gracious relationship, a healing, transforming gracious relationship. The first phrase of the familiar Trinitarian Benediction was no high-blown disembodied metaphor. It sprang out of actual experience. The men who first used it knew what it meant. They did not invent it, they saw it embodied and demonstrated by Jesus in his relationship not only with his own disciples, but also in his relationship with

19

the despised and rejected of men. In his company they had experienced the Grace that was in Christ Jesus. The Divine Initiative is expressed in Grace and man is justified when he accepts the Grace that comes all the way to meet him.

# 3) Tools for the Job

*'Be ye therefore wise as serpents, and harmless
as doves.'*                                    Matthew 10:16

JESUS is commissioning his disciples to go out into a
hostile world. With brutal frankness he warns them as
to what lies in store for them. 'You'll find yourselves in
collision with the power structures of the day, the
established authorities, the pressure of public opinion
and the crushing weight of the majority. Before these
forums you'll have to testify to One destined for crucifixion. To the serious and the snobs a nonentity. To
the intellectuals a scandal and a squalid blasphemy.'

Translate the language of the first century into contemporary idiom and the same devastating realism is
demanded of theologian and preacher alike. Standing
before a congress of philosophers, insisting on intellectual honesty; before the Gestapo deifying brute-force;
before the common man impervious to words like
judgement and grace, Christians need as much fortitude
now as they did on the even of their first commissioning.

No wonder these perplexed disciples trembled in face
of the task allotted to them. But they were by no means
the first to do this. So it was with the prophet Elijah
crying under the juniper tree, 'It is enough I can't cope'.
So it was with Isaiah shocked by the very suggestion
of a summons, 'But I am a man of unclean lips'. So it
was with Jeremiah protesting hotly 'But I am too

young'. The Bible supplies us with a whole battery of arguments against the agonizing demands of proclamation.

This understandable human inhibition goes hand in hand with the divine promise. To the prophets as they went forth against their own will, the pledge was given, 'My word shall not return unto me void'. And to the disciples fearful of the future Jesus gave the assurance, 'It shall be given you what to say'. 'It is not ye that speak but the spirit of the Father that dwelleth in you.' In other words when they joined battle with the enemy they found they were not alone in the field.

Quite so, but promises can be frightening too and there have been moments when men of God have fled from them. There is the God who is so unconditional in his demands. There is the fulfilment that beckons us from afar. There is the trustworthiness I must test and the verification on which I must stake my life. Yes, but he who trembles thus is experiencing a creative terror and this always is the mark of authentic preaching.

Why has preaching fallen on evil days? In some quarters it has so decayed and disintegrated that it is almost dead. How do we account for this *malaise*? Is it due to the competing interests and rival appeals of an affluent society? Is it due to the changing social structures which have shifted the centre of existence from personal relationship to the world of work? Or is it that the Church has lagged behind scientific progress, contemptuous of cultural change? The *malaise* of preaching, I believe, lies deeper. It is rooted in the pathological condition of our Christian witness to-day.

It is as if we had sent out reconnaissance troops to

search out the cause of the *malaise* of Christian proclamation—diagnosticians of the spirit of the times, *avantgardists* of every kind, sociologists, depth psychologists, clever boys who know how to get at people. Now it can't be denied that the experts will find much that is out of order, that here and there the dust of centuries will rise up where they have poked around. But these solemn analysts at the end of their sweaty efforts have missed the real cause. They are like a doctor describing an ugly wart but overlooking the deadly cancer underneath. As long as we remain blind to the 'sickness unto death' at the heart of Christian existence, all secondary remedies are meaningless. They are no more than innocuous symptom therapy.

On the eve of their first commissioning Jesus gave his disciples two clear injunctions.

(1) The first 'Be ye wise as serpents'. To put it more contemporaneously he enjoins all who profess him as Lord to exercise their capacity for critical reflection.

There are those who believe the Church will retrieve the ground she has lost by a return to what they prefer to call the simple gospel. From the catacombs of intellectual isolationism, they sally forth to christianize the world by the truculent reiteration of the old old story. The simple Gospellers despise the insights of science, philosophy, even theology. Guilty of oversimplifying issues that are maddeningly complex, they sell the pass to all enemies of the faith.

If preaching is in a sad state one reason perhaps is that it has not been cross-fertilized by theology, or that it has been rendered unbearably dull and boring by the wrong kind of theology—the esoteric scholasticism of the pundits. My late colleague and friend Ronnie Gregor

23

Smith used to say to his students 'You should go out of this place not as pseudo sociologists or as bogus psychologists but as theologians'. And of course Ronnie was right. The parish minister properly trained is the theologian in the field relating men's belief in God to what is happening in the community around them.

But wait, you say! With what school of theology do you want me to cross-fertilize my preaching? Aren't the traditional systems of theology in shambles? In dragging theology into the pulpit am I not more likely to become an agent of confusion than one of light? To be sure the time-honoured systems have been thrown into the melting pot but the God we proclaim has never been bound to any one system of philosophy or theology.

> *Our little systems have their day:*
> *They have their day and cease to be :*
> *They are but broken lights of Thee,*
> *And Thou, O Lord, art more than they.*

We must subject all systems of thought to fierce scrutiny including that of secular humanism. God meets us not on systems, but in the wonder and ambiguity of man's life in the world. This awareness is clarified by our experience in the Christian community that witnesses to Jesus Christ.

Anyhow in marrying theology and preaching to each other we find ourselves in good company—in that of Augustine, Luther and Calvin; in that of Karl Barth whose theology was born out of his preaching; in that of Niebuhr and Tillich. Strange that both these men, difficult to read theologically, were popular preachers.

24

They spoke to packed congregations everywhere they went. In that of D. M. Baillie, I recall vividly how often he would turn round from the lectern and on the blackboard with a piece of chalk write down the bones of a sermon—a model of simplicity and lucidity. Proclamation and critical reflection we must on no account divorce, for what God hath joined together let not man put asunder.

(2) Jesus on the eve of commissioning his disciples gave them a second injunction. He commanded them to be 'as harmless as doves', or to put it another way to exercise their capacity for love.

We may be as wise as serpents, as profound as Plato, as brilliant as Bertrand Russell, but if as Christians we do not communicate goodwill, we'll not be taken seriously. A few years ago the Americans coined the phrase 'the credibility gap'. It referred to the chasm that stretched between President Johnson's promises and his performance and the wider the chasm yawned the more cynical the American electorate became. Which is a parable of the dichotomy at the heart of Christian existence today.

Our world is full of functionaries, of propagandists, of paid purveyors of opinion, whose public creed is quite different from their private convictions. One sometimes gets the macabre impression that whether they are politicians or advertising experts they are no more than skilful manipulators. Animated by remote control they are only ventriloquists whose shrill voices echo the wishes of others.

But the preacher of the word is not a psycho-strategist. He must communicate credibility. If he dares to preach 'grace' he must endeavour to be gracious in his relationship with other people, even his enemies. If he summons up courage to preach on reconciliation, there are times he must pick up a phone, write a letter, ring a bell and say 'I am sorry' and mean it. What the druggist thinks in his heart does not sabotage the effectiveness of the cough mixture he so enthusiastically recommends. But the preacher is altogether different. The jealousies, the resentments, the hatreds, that smoulder in his heart, soon become voices that shout from the house tops. They rob him of his credibility.

Luther was tormented by one question, 'How can I find a gracious God?' This is the sort of question that is never asked in a restaurant or a pub to-day. But while this is so, people are curious to know what a man looks like who assiduously proclaims a message of salvation. In this age of alienation there is a deep longing for credibility. A man may be odd and eccentric but provided he tries to practise what he preaches, he is taken seriously.

There were millions of people who did not know that Albert Schweitzer was a great musician and a creative theologian. But the fact that he gave up a promising career to lance the disgusting abscesses of negroes in a jungle—this had a tremendous fascination —even for those who looked on his mission as out of date, and on his hospital as a dubious example of hygiene.

In his autobiography Berdyaev, the philosopher, claims that extravagant acts of human love constitute the credibility currency of Christianity. He cites the case of Mother Maria. When the Nazis were liquidating Jews in their gas chambers, one distraught mother refused to part with her baby. The officer in charge was only interested in the correct numerical returns so Mother Maria, without a word, pushed the mother aside and quietly took her place.

Don't get me wrong please. I am not arguing for what H. G. Wells called 'a scarifying asceticism', or for an amiable sentimentality, but for Christian love which is as costly now as ever it was. Christian witness that is credible calls not for cleverness, but it calls for purity—not for a plurality of passions but for what Kierkegaard describes as 'the purity to will one thing'. Except a grain of wheat fall into the ground and die it shall not bear fruit. Only he who dies and rises again with Christ in costly love can credibly bear witness to Him as Lord of Life and conqueror of death.

*This sermon was preached at the Ordination of the Revd Dr George Newlands, Glasgow University.*

# 4) The Need to Communicate

*'If the trumpet give an uncertain sound, who shall prepare himself to the battle?'*

1 Corinthians 14:8

THE typical twentieth century Christian finds this chapter somewhat puzzling. Speaking with tongues seems to us to be a grotesque pastime. Not so the first-century Christians. With them 'glossalalia'—the name they had for this phenomenon—was fairly common. In the course of prayer or meditation a man was caught up into some sort of ecstacy, and he proceded to pour out a cataract of sounds, conforming to no known syntax resembling no recognizable language.

The gift was highly coveted in the early Church. Those who possessed it enjoyed a special kind of distinction. Because the phenomenon was abnormal, they felt they were a cut above the average run of Christians. Not surprisingly the practice lent itself to spiritual pride and vulgar exhibitionism. This, coupled with the confusion it engendered, made Paul condemn it in no uncertain manner.

We may feel that Paul is making heavy weather of something which to us is so plainly absurd. But what the Apostle is really doing is pleading for intelligibility. If the event of Christ is so stupendously significant, as we claim it is, then we must broadcast it as clearly as we know how. Ambiguity either in content or communication of the message leads in the end to loss of nerve and total paralysis. 'If the trumpet give an uncertain sound who shall prepare himself to the battle?'

These words speak to our condition. The traditional authorities that once undergirded our society have been repudiated. The moral landmarks that guided countless generations on their way have been obliterated and their place taken by the wobbly relativities of permissive ethics. The triumphant certainties which in former days sent men to the stake have been eroded. This has not happened overnight. It has advanced slowly and imperceptibly over many generations, gathering a furious momentum within the last decade. Matthew Arnold saw it coming:

> *The sea of faith*
> *Was once, too, at the full and round earth's shore*
> *Lay like the folds of a bright girdle furled*
> *But now I only hear*
> *Its melancholy, long withdrawing roar,*
> *Retreating to the breath*
> *Of the night wind, down the vast edges drear*
> *And naked shingles of the world.*

Before the gigantic issues of the day clamouring for an answer we stand dazed and stunned and bewildered. The problems of war, race, world hunger and universal anxiety neurosis no doubt demand study and analysis, but, above all, they are crying out for some word from the Lord. High above the tumult of the world's confusion and the babel of its conflicting ideologies certain notes should be heard sharp and insistent and im-

29

perious, for 'if the trumpet give an uncertain sound who shall prepare himself to the battle'.

We must speak unambiguously about man.

In an age when so many notable thinkers have pronounced God dead, the autonomy of man is being trumpeted on all sides. The celebration of this autonomy is not something that belongs distinctively to any one school of thought. It has found many different expressions, ranging from Bertrand Russell's 'foundation of unyielding despair' on the one hand to the most extravagant and buoyant forms of optimism on the other.

Sartre, the philosopher and novelist, argues that since God has been irrevocably buried, man is now in absolute control. Under no illusion whatsoever as to the intractable nature of the human dilemma, Sartre spurns any form of supernatural comfort. Life he asserts is basically meaningless. There is no structure of ultimate coherence, purpose or goodness anywhere in the universe. In this vacuum of belief, in this God-forsaken world, in a culture with a metaphysical void yawning at its centre, man is absolutely alone. He has only his own courage to forge whatever freedom of spirit there is within the brief span of years allotted to him on this planet.

At the other end of the spectrum we find William Hamilton, one of the younger radical American theologians. Man is in charge and does not need God any more, he writes with bubbling optimism. The world is not as cruel as the pessimists say and the contemporary godlessness is not a tragic fate. On the contrary, the world is a place of creative discovery, of constant reform, of emerging and expanding values. Christians should catch the modern mood from technological development, democratic protest, from song, dance and from, of course, the Beatles. This brand of optimism on the part of a theologian is surpassing strange when the most 'with it' secularistic movements, the New Left, the Hippies and Black Power have lost all faith in the democratic process.

This belief in man's ability to work out his own salvation is not confirmed by the facts of contemporary history. Is it sheer accident that in the most scientifically advanced countries there is a startling renaissance of astrology. Nor is it without significance that the increase in psychosomatic and mental diseases seem to be in direct proportion to the almost miraculous progress made by modern medicine. Whatever the hackneyed phrase 'come of age' means it does not look as if man can yet boast of being his own saviour. With the structures of reason and coherence collapsing all around him, and the ancient gods we thought were buried beginning to rise again, like the Philippian jailer in the middle of an earthquake, modern man is asking 'How can I be saved?'

What we need desperately is the recovery of the human centre, the reaffirmation of the biblical doctrine of the divine image. To lose this conviction is to lapse into anonymity and to surrender our identity. In its starkest sense it means to lose one's soul. Whenever this happens the real difference between man and animal disappears and whole societies fall into a patho-logical state of collectivity, ruled by all sorts of fears and fantasies. Hence the importance of emphasizing the full humanity of Jesus Christ. In him we see the true relationship between God and the world. In him transcendence and time meet. In him man's vocation to become a free and responsible being is revealed for all time.

Again we must speak unambiguously about God.

Some time ago I read a most fascinating novel by Ian Crichton Smith called *Consider the Lillies*. It is about the Highland clearances, surely one of the most unsavoury chapters in Scottish history. Absentee landlords, deciding sheep paid better than men, drove the people off the land, callously indifferent to their fate. The heroine of the novel is an old widow—Mrs Macdonald, who was served notice to quit her house within a fortnight. The moment the factor was out of sight she hurried to the minister but he tried to fob her off with the monstrous suggestion that this inhuman act was the will of God. When the cruch came she met it magnificently, but was not seen in church again. Skilfully the author leaves us to speculate whether the empty space in the customary pew was an act of calculated defiance, a vote of censure on the God, who in the words of H. G. Wells, proved 'an ever absent help in time of trouble'—the God who in the midst of her anguish remained as silent as the sphinx in the Egyptian desert.

It is our sacred duty to demolish any God who is insensitive to the human predicament. The time has come to declare war on the gods that still claim the allegiance of millions, the god of nationalism, the god of organized pleasure, the god of white supremacy. We must also do away with the cosmic fixer up, the magical father figure, the heavenly tranquillizer, helping to keep people docile. The abandoned altars of the gods that no longer serve human purpose litter history and over their departure we must shed no tears.

But the new trend is different. It is not the false conceptions, nor the out-moded theological images men are repudiating. They have made an assault of the God of the Bible himself. The novelists began the work of demolition long before the modern theologians had got round to it—Kafka, Hemingway, Camus and Sartre, a couple of decades before the Death of God boys got busy, wrote 'God is dead and the only decent thing to do with a corpse is to bury it'.

Then came the latter day morticians who have disposed of God but wax delirious about Jesus 'the man for others'. In what sense Christian atheism can be distinguished from humanism is difficult to see. The good humanist is prepared to suffer and indeed to die without adulation for 'the man for others'. There is the added difficulty that Jesus, unless the Gospels are deliberate fabrications, believed in God. He prayed to him, trusted in him, and with his last breath he committed himself to his care. Jesus may have been mistaken but if he was wrong in something so crucially important as this, is there any compelling reason why we should make him our model or call him 'the man for others'?

If the Christian atheists are right we can say good-bye to preaching. Is there anything to proclaim if we rule out from the creed the words 'I believe in God the Father Almighty'? Why urge people to worship if prayer is but another name for auto-suggestion? Why expect men and women to fight for social justice if there is no God whose Kingdom is an everlasting Kingdom?

To be sure, our minds must be open to new ways of thinking about God and new ways of describing him.

33

We may not care to describe him after the manner of the psalmist as the 'one who breaks the bow and cuts the spear asunder' but the same absolute conviction of God's involvement in human history must be ours too.

The Christian and the humanist can work together and can share a number of similar visions. But there is a very decisive difference. The humanist believes that his values have no reference beyond man himself. The Christian on the other hand affirms that his values are neither self-generating, nor self-perpetrating—they are grounded in the Reality we call God. And the Christian God is not a cosmic absentee landlord, insensitive to human need. He is like Jesus, who was no phantom deity moving through life untouched by the problems that tear the world apart. Jesus lived, suffered and died, not to draw attention to himself but to reveal that behind and beyond all things there was one whom he called Father. This note we must not muffle 'for if the trumphet give an uncertain sound who will prepare himself to the battle'.

Finally we must speak unambiguously about the Church.

All over the world there is a revolt against institutions and the Church is no exception. In America it is estimated that only 50 per cent of theological students opt for the parish ministry, and the incidence of drop-out among the ordained clergy, including Roman Catholic priests, is reaching alarming proportions. The same trend, slower and more hesitant, is discernible in Britain and in Germany.

There are those who castigate the drop-outs as cowardly deserters. They liken them to rats scurrying away from a sinking ship. In leaving the Church they are only rationalizing their own failure and inadequacy. But this sweeping condemnation is far from just. No doubt there are misfits in the ministry and we can be sure some of them have dropped out for the wrong reasons. This however is not the whole story. Among the ministers who have dropped out there are men who are remarkably sincere and intelligent and they have not taken the step lightly. Mistaken they may be, but they have left because they believe the institutional Church has become an embarrassing anachronism. They are convinced that God has chosen some other means to implement his purpose in history.

Whatever sympathy I can muster for such rebels I have none for Malcolm Muggeridge who has become the arch-apostle of an anti-institutional, disembodied anaemic religion. In his slim volume *Jesus Rediscovered* he says he accepts the historical fact of Christ as the God man and the crucifixion as the act and symbol of man's redemption. Then with equal enthusiasm he argues that the churches are major hindrances in the spread of Christianity. Muggeridge rejects all ecclesiastical structures and takes a wry delight in what he believes to be their imminent dissolution.

There are two questions I would like to ask Muggeridge if someone could arrange a confrontation on television. Did not Jesus gather round himself a band of apostles, the nucleus, the prototype of the Church that was to be? Did he not intend this community to be the flesh and blood of the spirit? And anyhow, how did Muggeridge arrive at his knowledge of Jesus whom he acknowledges as the God man? Was it not through the Church? The thing we must never be allowed to forget is that it was the Church, not her critics, that wrote the Gospels which tell us of Jesus. It was the Church that preserved them with her blood, and passed them on to the succeeding generations of the children of men.

The institutional Church may have failed lamentably, but we can't dispense with her. Every worthwhile belief under the sun must put on flesh and blood, must take to itself a body. Democracy will ever remain a dream till it embodies itself in a political structure, call it what you will, House of Commons, Congress, United Nations. Education will be only a beckoning hope—no more, till it becomes incarnate in a village school, in an institution we call a university, in books and libraries, in scholars bristling with peculiar eccentricities. Similarly with the Christian faith. Unless it assumes flesh and blood in the shape of an institution it will evaporate into a mere nostalgic memory.

By all means let us discard the ecclesiastical structures that no longer serve a useful purpose. Let us do away with any organization that impedes the coming of the Kingdom of God on earth, but when all is said and done we cannot dispense with the institution. The Churches are fallible, says Tillich, but they are bearers of the Divine. This conviction we can't suppress for here 'if the trumpet give an uncertain sound who will prepare himself to the battle?'

# 5) The Judgement of Christ

> *'Inasmuch as ye have done it unto one of the least of these my brethren, ye have done it unto me.'*　　　　　　　Matthew 25 : 40

LONG before Jesus was born in Bethlehem the Greeks believed in judgement, only they called it nemesis. A man might convince himself he could break all the canons of morality with impunity, but he was only deceiving himself. Already the avenging furies were hot on his track, sniffing at his heels. In the end they always succeeded in catching up with him.

Modern man, however sceptical, is prepared to conceded that such a law does exist. He has learned from bitter experience that conduct cannot be divorced from its consequences. He knows that drunkenness invites disaster, than lying forfeits confidence, that selfishness, no matter how cunningly disguised, is stultifying and self-defeating. He may not believe in God, but he is at least inclined to say Amen to one New Testament affirmation, 'Whatsoever a man soweth, that shall he also reap.'

That Jesus believed in judgement is beyond any doubt. His conviction regarding the moral nature of the universe throbs at the heart of some of his great parables. Dives and Lazarus, the man who built bigger barns and had not reckoned with death, the inevitable fate that overtook the house that was empty, swept and

37

garnished, to mention only a few. Remove the element of judgement from the teaching of Jesus and we have not only misconstrued it, we have in fact mutilated it out of all possible recognition.

Here in the parable of the Sheep and the Goats, Jesus, the master artist, with a few deft strokes, paints for us a picture of the meaning of divine judgement. Read it through and your first reaction is one of puzzled surprise. There is no reference to a creed. Those on trial are not charged with any crime. They are not even accused of having broken a single commandment. What strikes you is the reasonableness of the test applied. The criterion seems to be one of ordinary down-to-earth, no-nonsense kindness—feeding the hungry, clothing the naked, visiting those in prison. It is the sort of thing many humanists, as well as Christians sponsor in their crusades for the disinherited of this earth.

Indeed the parable seems to offer tons of ammunition to the sceptic. 'Isn't this what I have been saying all along!' he shouts. It's the way a man behaves that counts, not what he believes. This world of ours, riddled with want and injustice, cries out not for a stratospheric theology but for a down-to-earth practical humanitarianism. 'Love thy neighbour as thyself.' That is the only commandment that makes sense to the contemporary mind and the only one that can command unswerving allegiance.

A superficial reading of the parable may appear to support such an interpretation, but a more thorough-going examination shows that its challenge goes far beyonds the bounds of mere human decency. Under its searchlight our own grubby selfishness stands mercilessly exposed. Even the saints themselves fall far short of its exacting standards. In this parable we find that those who are condemned fall into three main groups which are as familiar to us to-day as they were in first-century Palestine.

## The first group are the complacent

The parable makes it clear that those who were actually condemned thought they were good enough, while those who passed muster were visibly surprised that they were accepted. This insight of Jesus focuses for us the profound paradox of moral experience. The less good, as Niebuhr again and again reminds us, are characterized by a complacent conscience. 'They do not lie awake at night and fret over their sins.' The spiritually sensitive on the other hand are tormented by a sense of their own unworthiness. Jesus could not stand complacent people. That is why he lashed the religious establishment of his day with cutting invective. 'Ye serpents, ye generation of vipers—ye whited sepulchres.' Blistering language! In our protocol-conscious British society he would definitely have been sued for libel. Be that as it may the complacent are as thick on the ground to-day as they were when Jesus expounded this parable.

We meet the complacent inside the Church, massed battalions of them; worshippers of a sanctified *status quo*, tenacious defenders, not of a dynamic faith, but of moribund institutions, obsolete theologies, discredited patterns of evangelism. In my former church, St George's West, Edinburgh, we launched an evangelistic experiment, which among other things, included games and dancing in the crypt of the church. The first evening we were picketed by Bible-brandishing

Christians, bristling with self-righteousness. Few of us are guilty perhaps of such crude behaviour. We pride ourselves on our broad-mindedness, on our emancipation from crippling orthodoxies; on our smooth adjustment to contemporary fads and fashions, but behind the liberal façade there lurk a number of ferocious prejudices. And we are prepared to fight like tigers to retain privilege.

But the complacent are not confined to the Church. Pharisaism is not an occupational disease of the devout and the orthodox, it is a universal *malaise*. Ask the neo-pagan of to-day why he is so contemptuous of the Church, and uses it as a mere convenience, and his answer invariably reflects the depth of his complacency. He can ignore the Church, he claims, because without the benefit of prayer or faith he can cope with life, tolerably well on his own. This attitude is summed up in one of his essays by the late Professor J. B. S. Haldane. He writes: 'I do not claim to be a saint, but I am not a bad man. I fancy I may be better than many who call themselves Christians.'

He may very well be, but he has no right to say so. The strange thing about the genuine saint is that he really believes he is a bad man. Like those who passed the test in the parable, he is surprised that anyone should ever call him good. It is becoming increasingly clear that this is not an easy-going parable, parading a trite moral. Its insights judge us in the deep places of our being.

*The second group are the socially selective*

Those who passed the gruelling test were all-inclusive in their sympathy. This was a pre-condition of their acceptance. Their compassion was not limited to their own family or to a select circle of friends; it reached out to the despised and rejected of men. 'Inasmuch as ye have done it unto the least of these my brethren, ye have done it unto me.'

I can understand why the Establishment ganged up on Jesus and engineered his destruction. He committed the unpardonable crime of crashing into their cosy, well-regulated world and reversing their scale of values. He had the effrontery to teach that social outcasts like publicans and prostitutes were nearer the Kingdom of Heaven than the accredited leaders of religion. Imagine the steep rise in their blood pressure when they heard these outrageous words, 'And the first shall be last and the last shall be first.' What Professor Niebuhr calls 'a transvaluation of values'.

His parable is very severe on those whom we are apt to describe as 'nice people'. Somehow or other conventional Christians and humanists have convinced themselves that 'niceness' is the supreme goal of all moral ambition, that it is an adequate substitute for God himself. Far worse is the blasphemous selectiveness of our niceness. We approve of those who are like us, who dress like us, speak like us, and support the self-same causes. We are even prepared to approve of those whom we regard as our social inferiors, as long as they are willing to acknowledge our innate superiority. And what Jesus is saying in the parable is something like this. 'I am not impressed by the cult of niceness. It is easy to be civilized to those you approve of; but what about the misfits of society, the riff-raff, the scum, the submerged element who have given up trying? What about the rebels, the noisy radicals, the juvenile delinquents and the hard-bitten criminals? Are you prepared to be nice to them? You say you believe in the Fatherhood of God', says Jesus, 'but do you? What does such a creed mean when you are prepared to sponsor a policy of racial segregation, and refuse to let your children be educated with those who come from underprivileged homes'. 'In asmuch as ye have done it to the least of these, my brethren.' The key word is 'least'. It stabs us to the quick and pierces through all our spurious rationalizations and subterfuges. It reminds us that we all stand under the judgement of Christ.

If we had stood on the quay of the seaport of Carthageria in the year 1650, we would have witnessed the following spectacle. A slave ship with hordes of tightly packed, sweating negroes, battened down under the hatches, is being tied up. The moment the holds are opened, a putrefying stench, scatters the people on the pier. But there is one man standing there who doesn't turn his back. The instant the ropes are secured, he leaps aboard and disappears into the bowels of the ship. For the next three days he works like a demon; a bit of tobacco here, a sip of brandy there, a festering core cleaned and bandaged. That is how Peter Claver the saint served his Master. In this world he received little recognition, but in the next he will hear himself addressed: 'Come ye blessed of my Father—inherit the Kingdom prepared for you from the foundation of the earth . . . for as much as you have done it to the least of these my brethren ye have done it unto me.'

I suppose I am as guilty as most of the sin of social selectiveness but in my best moments I hate it. At such times I know that no amount of clever sophistry on my part can square it with the basic Christian doctrine 'The Fatherhoood of God.

### The third group that stands under judgement is the uncommitted spectators

Read the parable and the most startling thing is the grounds of the rejection of the guilty. They were condemned not for committing crimes against humanity, not for moral misdemeanour, not for holding heretical beliefs. They were condemned not for doing anything but for doing nothing. They were judged because they sat in the grandstand, dilettante, detached spectators, refusing to get involved.

The parable makes it plain that faith and action are inseparable. If a man genuinely believes, he is prepared to get involved. If he is not willing to get involved, it means he lacks conviction. Running through the New Testament is this insistence in a clear-cut decisiveness— the taking of an unequivocal stand—the moving over from the realm of argument to that of commitment. 'Not everyone that sayeth unto me Lord, Lord shall enter into the Kingdom of Heaven but he that doeth the will of my Father which is in Heaven.'

It is at least arguable that we see the judgement of God upon our world to-day in the shape of Communism. And the most disturbing thing about Communism is not its technical know-how but its decisiveness, its possession of a goal and its determination to press towards it with all the resources at its command.

When Whittaker Chambers stood trial before the Committee on Un-American Activities a cross-examining counsel asked, 'What does it mean to be a Communist?' Chambers thought for a moment and then answered, 'When I was a Communist I had three heroes. The first was a Russian named Sazanov. In a camp in Siberia he drenched himself in kerosene and was burned to death in an effective protest against the way the camp was being run. The second was a Pole called Derjinskey. Erudite and cultured as few were, he insisted on cleaning out the lavatories on the basis that the leader must undertake the lowliest tasks. The third was a Jew known as Levine. When the court-martial that tried him sentenced him to death, he smiled like a Christian martyr and remarked serenely "we Communists are always under sentence of death".' 'That', concluded Chambers, 'is what it means to be a Communist'.

Our universities, on the other hand, are turning out thousands of graduates—future leaders of our society who don't seem to believe anything—'in whom the native hue of resolution is sickled o'er by the pale cast of thought'. It is like an inverse ratio sum. The more educated a man is, the less conviction he appears to have about anything. It is this indecisiveness not the Hydrogen bomb that threatens the future of Western civilization.

The Russian philosopher Nicholas Berdyaev writes, 'There is no longer any room in the world for a merely external form of Christianity based upon custom. Our world is entering upon a period of catastrophe and crisis when we are being forced to take sides, and in which a higher and more intense kind of spiritual life will be demanded of Christians'. In other words, we must begin to take the phrase 'Decision for Christ' seriously. On no account must we leave it to intinerant evangelists who devalue it by divorcing it from the intellect and the robust creative vitalities of our nature. We must preach it, unselfconsciously, restoring to it its original New Testament meaning. Decision for Christ is not an emotional experience—a mixture of asterisks and hysterics. It is rather a painful revolution, carrying with it the disturbing, radical implications this parable so provocatively portrays.

# 6) Anatomy of Humility

*'He that findeth his life shall lose it: and he
that loseth his life for my sake shall find it.'*
Matthew 10:39

THESE words of Jesus are found, with only slight
variations, in the four gospels. Therefore we can con-
clude that they made a deep impression on the thinking
of the early Church. They seem to imply that there is
a law embedded in the very nature of things, more
immutable than gravity itself—a law which decrees that
preoccupation with self is stultifying and self-defeating,
whereas self-forgetfulness results in a sense of release
and fulfilment.

Perhaps one of the most overworked words in the
English language at the moment is the word 'image'.
But no matter how hackneyed it has become, we are
not able to dispense with it altogether. Image projection
has developed into a major industry, in whose service
some of our ablest brains and latest techniques of
publicity are employed.

Communism, despite its massive strength, by no
means underestimates the importance of projecting a
pleasing image of itself. Hence the fabulous sums of
money it is prepared to spend on propaganda, posing
as the champion of the disinherited, and the emanci-
pator of all who are suppressed. Napoleon's cynical
assertion that God is on the side of the biggest battalion

they would rephrase into 'God smiles on the most pleasing image'.

In the Democracies, the projection of an acceptable image is the concern of all parties contending for political power. The late President Kennedy with his youthful panache and infectious idealism succeeded not only in getting into the White House, but also in riveting the attention of the whole world. In Britain the impression the party leader manages to create, through the media of press and television, is all decisive.

And the Church, whatever she thinks of this over-worked word, can't afford to dissociate herself from it. Whether she knows it or not, she is projecting an image of herself on the public screen—an image which conditions the attitude of the masses and the response of individuals to the message she is commissioned to proclaim. At the moment it would appear that the only image of Christianity the Church succeeds in projecting is one of hopeless distortion.

The truth is that the distortion of the Christian image began in New Testament times, till by the fifth century AD it had become a grotesque kind of caricature. By then, the ideal Christian had come to be looked upon as one who had turned his back on the world, someone who had renounced all its legitimate interests and pleasures, someone who had buried himself in a monastery or a hermit cell, where he could cultivate his soul in solitude and seculsion.

A striking example of this distortion of the Christian image is found in Paulinus of Nola, a Roman patrician, a millionaire, a cultured poet, a governor of a province and a senator before the age of thirty. He was converted to Christianity and what did he do? Did he use his social and political prestige to commend the newly-found faith to his peers? Did he dedicate his poetic talents to exalt the Saviour he now professed? Did he exercise his immense influence to try and stem the rot in the public life of Rome, to avert the nemesis so soon to overtake it? Not at all. Paulinus came to terms with the Christian image that had by now imposed itself on many of the most discerning minds of his day. He disappeared from public life and his letters went unanswered. After four years' complete silence, he was at last tracked down in monastic seclusion in Spain. There he spent his money on ransoming prisoners, and when at length his wealth was exhausted, he sold himself into slavery in order to ransom a widow's son. No one, not even the crassest cynic can fail to be impressed by this man's conduct. Still the question remains, is this the kind of behaviour Jesus expects of His followers?

Protestants do not believe in a life-denying religion, nor do they attach much importance to monastic seclusion. But over the centuries they have succeeded in creating an image of Christian humility which in some respects is even more damaging than a headlong flight from the world. I don't mean the Uriah Heep kind of humility which is one of the crudest of all Dickens' caricatures. It is easy to see through the Uriah Heeps of our society and to demolish them with the contempt they deserve. It is far more difficult when a man is an admirable character like Paulinus of Nola, the walking, living embodiment of what passes for traditional Christian humility.

We would all agree that a Christian is a man marked by genuine humility, but has it ever occurred to us that the stereotyped humility, most of us admire, is in all essentials a false one? In all the big political and social issues demanding involvement, he is found sitting on the fence and prone to be straddled thereon. Ask the average church member to describe the picture of a humble man he hangs up in his mental gallery, and does it not go somewhat like this? He is meek, modest and unobtrusive. A lover of the back seat and a hater of the limelight, you look in vain for him in any fiercely contested arena of controversy. And the universal verdict is 'He hasn't an enemy in the world', and, according to his women friends, 'a real pet'. This, I submit, is the popular picture of the humble man. If this conception is the true one, I am afraid we'll have to part company with some of the most disturbing characters of all time.

We'll have to part company with Paul, the greatest Christian in history. His humility is beyound doubt. Did he not once describe himself as the least of all saints and the greatest of all sinners? Yes, but there was nothing neutral and innocuous about him either. Never out of trouble, he made it his business to expose and attack every kind of sanctified iniquity. When Jewish Christians refused to eat at the same tables with Gentile Christians, Peter abjectly acquiesced. I suppose he rationalized, as we all do. It is tradition. Everybody expects it and there is no point in being awkward. But Paul would have none of it. He deliberately forced the issue and by being utterly uncompromising, he saved Christianity from becoming a minor sect of Judaism.

Furthermore we'll have to part company with Luther, the great Reformer. No wonder his enemies called him the turbulent monk. Turbulent. That's too mild a word. He should be rechristened 'Martin Dynamite Luther'.

He must have been tempted to cultivate his soul in sequestered anonymity, away from the surge and thunder of the outside world. Instead, he nailed his 95 theses provocatively and aggressively to the door of Wittenberg church, and thereby launched a revolution whose reverberations are still felt in our midst.

Above all, if the popular conception of humility is the correct one, we must part company with Jesus himself. His was a humility of which the manger cradle is the initial symbol; and the Cross, bleak upon the hill, the inevitable climax. But he also made enemies and aroused the most savage opposition. The old liberal picture of Jesus, as an amiable carpenter, spinning memorable stories and rhapsodizing about birds of the air and lilies of the field, while he dispensed wholesale benevolence all around him, will not stand close scrutiny. Much nearer the truth is the picture H. G. Wells gives of him as a rugged hunter, digging mankind out of the snug burrows of their habitual complacency. The Jesus of the Gospels was more than meek and lowly of heart. He was a no-quarter controversialist who did not hesitate to call in question the most sacred traditions and to speak and act in place of God himself.

An examination of the great personalities of the Bible points us in the direction of one incontrovertible fact. Christian humility is something very different from a carefully cultivated obsequiousness, a studied unobtrusiveness, a diffused amiableness whose motto is 'peace at any price'. No, it is rather the by-product of a divine obsession, so that the ego, with its devouring demands, ceases to count, and God becomes all in all. Humility finds its highest expression in Christ's own prayer in Gethsemane—'Not my will but Thine be done'.

Christian theology has consistently claimed that the No. 1 sin is not animal sensuality, but human pride. And what is pride but self-adulation, the elevation of our own ambitions above the needs of others, the enthroning of the ego in the place which belongs only to God? In men like Napoleon and Hitler, egotism reached pathological proportions, but in all of us it is deep-seated, defying our most strenuous efforts at dislodgement.

And egotism is a past-master in the art of disguise. There are those who speak in accents of meekness and unpretentiousness when all the time they are in the grip of demonic ambition. There are others who deplore strife, but they are bogus peacemakers motivated by the fear that their precious ego may get mauled and battered in the arena of fierce controversy. And don't tell me that egotism is curbed by education. Those who labour under this particular brand of illusion are not familiar with the back-room intrigues and cut-throat jealousies that go on at a university. To disenchant themselves, let them read the novels of C. P. Snow.

Nor is egotism conquered by asceticism or any amount of mortification of the flesh. Once, runs the old story, there was a religious hermit, so holy that the evil spirits sent to tempt him were defeated. They tried the passions of his body and failed. They tried the doubts of his mind and again failed. They could not break him down. Then Satan himself took over and to the evil spirits said, 'Your methods have been too crude. Permit me a moment'. Then, going up to the hermit, Satan said, 'Have you heard the good news. Your friend has been made Bishop of Alexandria'. Whereupon the holy man ground his teeth in anger and jealousy. No, Egotism is never dead, not even with the most dedicated and devout.

There are Christians who strive after spiritual perfectionism, on the basis of the proof text, 'Be ye perfect, even as your Father which is in Heaven is perfect'. Weakness in any shape or form is anathema to them and, in order to eradicate it, they are prepared to go to any extreme. The truth is that perfectionism is born of egotism. It is a refusal to accept the self with all the inevitable shortcomings, a failure to recognize that there are certain temptations and tensions we can never quite overcome in this world. It is the secret wish to be like God himself, perfect and without blemish, which is pride at its deadliest. If we would be healthy psychologically and indeed spiritually, we must come to terms with the fact that sin is part and parcel of human nature, and can never be completely eradicated.

What then is the cure of egotism, the universal legacy we all have a share in, the worst cancer that defies every form of surgery, however ruthless? It is not education. It is not ascetism. And it is certainly not the self-conscious cultivation of the spiritual life. These exercises serve only to sanctify and strengthen it. In the end there is only one answer to the egotism that bedevils us all; the abandoning of ourselves to a worthwhile cause, the giving of our allegiance to someone who makes unconditional demands upon us. And for us there is only one way—surrender to Jesus Christ; and the acceptance of all the radical implications this act of obedience entails. What is the secret of humility? Jesus gives it to us in these profound and paradoxical words, 'He that findeth his life shall lose it, and he that loseth his life for my sake shall find it'.

Let us then follow Christ with singleness of mind and with undeviating purpose, and I wager the world will not praise us for our meekness. Far more likely it will accuse us of aggressiveness, but in the measure in which we lose ourselves in him, we shall exhibit in our lives the grace of Christian humility and at the same time experience the Peace of God that passeth all understanding.

# 7) Anatomy of Christian Comfort

> *'How shall we sing the Lord's song in a strange land?'*    Psalm 137:4
> *'Comfort ye, comfort ye my people, saith your God.'*    Isaiah 40:1

THIS haunting question was asked by men who had languished in exile for fifty years. Uprooted from their own native land, separated from the symbols of their religion, overwhelmed by the weight of a pagan culture, their morale was at a low ebb. But what really hurt them most was not their bondage nor the taunts of their tormentors, but a devastating sense of God-forsakenness. They believed that God was localized in Jerusalem and that he was powerless to help them in far-off Babylon. To these ancient Hebrews God was not dead, he was simply impotent, a quaint anachronism, a symbol of the good old days, remembered with nostalgia and homesickness.

Is not this a fairly accurate picture of the contemporary situation? Behind every crisis that bombards us, the crisis of youth, the crisis of crime, the crisis of corroding values, there lurks the real crisis—that of Belief. We are witnessing what Buber calls the eclipse of the supernatural, man's inability to see that God plays any significant role in what is happening in our world today.

Not for a moment do I want to play down the enormity of the problems that haunt us, the cult of violence, the collapse of morals, the preoccupation with sex, drugs and all kinds of perversions. They not only call for attention, they also demand positive legislation, but in themselves these problems are but visible symptoms of the deeper *malaise* that affects society. They are the palliatives, trying to dull the ache of the inner terror, the sense of meaninglessness which according to Tillich is the special dread of our age.

And the answer to this deadly *malaise*? Has Billy Graham got it with his message of atomic apocalypticism, his warning of a Sodom and Gomorrah judgement on this sinful generation in the shape of a nuclear holocaust? Or have the apostles of repressive legislation got it, proferring their own panaceas—bring back the birch, bring back hanging, get rid of the lesser breeds outwith the law and become more British.

If the diagnosis of the contemporary dilemma I am offering you is anywhere near the truth, if the real *malaise* is anxiety, stemming from a sense of God-forsakenness, then Isaiah's answer is the right one—'comfort ye, comfort ye my people, saith your God'. What a profound insight into the meaning of the human predicament. When men experience lostness and estrangement, when they are sunk so deep in the pit of despair, that they can't pull themselves out, there isn't much point in condemning them for their sins, or castigating them for their faithlessness. What they need above all is a sense of comfort, the assurance that behind the seeming chaos and cruel indifference there is a meaning which makes sense of all our strivings. And by comfort I mean not religion as dope, not religion as mother's soothing syrup, not religion as a psychological shot in the arm, but religion as fortitude. This is the true meaning of comfort which derives from the little Latin word *fors* meaning strength. What then are the bones that stick out in the anatomy of Christian comfort?

1) *Comfort springs from the assurance that God can't finally be defeated*

The ancient Jews found it difficult to square a belief in a God who had chosen them to serve his purpose in history, with the cruel exile they were now experiencing by the alien waters of Babylon. If God was the Lord of history, if he controlled the destinies of men and nations, and was capable of intervening in human affairs, why was he neutral when Judah was overrun, Jerusalem sacked, thousands slaughtered and the *élite* of the land carried away into bondage in foreign parts? Bafflement and a profound sense of sadness can be heard in the haunting cry 'How shall we sing the Lord's song in a strange land?'

This is an ever recurring problem. Since the last war many of our novels and plays wrestle with this theme— the neutrality of God. The Governor of the universe seems to have abdicated and to have left his throne to psychopathic dictators with demonic pretensions. This is the theme of a play by a German poet by the name of Borchert which he calles 'Outside the door'. God appears in the guise of a weeping old man, wringing his hands helplessly over the sufferings and the follies of the human race. The hero of the play is a German soldier called Beckmann who had miraculously survived the hell of Stalingrad.

56

'I can do nothing', says God. 'Just so', Beckmann replies, 'you can do nothing'. 'We do not fear you any more. We do not love you any more . . . you speak low at the present, too low for the thunder of our time. We cannot hear you any more.'

This German poet, along with a number of contemporary theologians, brings us face to face with a question it is not possible to side-step. Once circumstances force us to acknowledge that our own infantile strivings are doomed to failure the question of God inevitably arises. If man himself is not the source of a deathless and victorious power, is there any such power? Is there any force, mind or person working at the heart of things, to bring order out of chaos, meaning out of chance, triumph out of tragedy? Or is history a tale told by an idiot?

In his little book *Rumour of Angels* the American sociologist Peter Berger supplies us with an excellent illustration of what Christian comfort really means, all the more telling because the one he uses is so ordinary and basic to life. A child wakes up in the night and finds himself in the dark, beset by nameless threats. The contours of trusted reality have become blurred and in terror the child cries for his mother. In his little mind she possesses the power to banish chaos and minister comfort. And this she proceeds to do. Taking the child and cradling him in her arms, she turns on a lamp, filling the room with a warm glow of reassuring light. She will speak to the child and whatever the words the message she imparts is this, 'Don't be afraid; everything is in order—everything is all right'. The child is comforted, his trust in ordered reality recovered and he goes back to sleep.

Berger's point is that this parental comfort points beyond itself to a deathless love that broods at the very heart of the universe. If there isn't such a fact, then all our efforts at comforting one another belong to the world of illusion. Freud was right. Religion is the childish fantasy that there is some cosmic parent that runs the universe for our benefit. And so the nightmare of chaos, not the assurance of a universal purpose running through all things, is the final truth about the human situation. The meaning of Christian comfort is very different. Human experience may supply evidence which at best is only ambiguous, pointing to the finality of death and the triumph of evil. Nevertheless the man of faith trusts in a God who conserves the meanings created within history and mysteriously brings them to fulfilment.

2) *Comfort springs out of the assurance that God can't be domesticated*

The Jews of the Old Testament, prior to the exile, thought they had thoroughly domesticated God. Localized in Jerusalem, the capital city, imprisoned in the temple, trapped in the holy of holies, pushed far back behind a massive curtain, he was accessible only to the high priest and that only once a year. They assumed that God was their exclusive property. They had him placed, fixed and cornered for all time.

We no longer localize God in one country or in one sanctuary, but while paying lip service to the doctrine of his omnipresence we still try to domesticate him. The methods we use to manipulate God may be more sophisticated than those used by Isaiah's contemporaries but they are not all that subtle either.

We use God to sanctify all sorts of monstrous iniquities. When Rhodesia, at the height of the independence crisis, rejected the proposals for negro majority rule agreed on by the major British political parties, Ian Smith, the Prime Minister, broadcast a message to the nation. He advanced a number of reasons why Rhodesia had decided to go independent. One in particular I found very disconcerting. He blandly stated that a white minority had to retain power in order to preserve Christian civilization in that part of Africa. It just did not occur to him that he was guilty of blasphemy—the preservation of Christianity at the cost of brotherhood and justice; the subjugation of millions to perpetual servitude in the name of Jesus Christ.

And we are past masters at domesticating God religiously. Religious wars, the last word in ferocity and cruelty, were the products of particular ecclesiastical politics. God, the creator of the ends of the earth, had to be thought of in one way and one way only, and freedom of worship was denied. Roman Catholics conceived of him as a cosmic Pope issuing sundry *ex cathedra* pronouncements. Anglicans assumed that anyone who ran the universe had to be an episcopalian. Presbyterians, while deploring the myth of apostolic succession, felt sure that the Almighty had arranged the writing of the Westminster Confession. Most of our ecumenical headaches at the present juncture stem from the hoary practice of domesticating God.

In our churches we have so domesticated God that it is difficult to see any difference between him and what we ourselves believe. God and our morals; God and our race; God and our vanities; God and our scruples are all one. So much so that the transcendent

One, the God of awe and majesty, has vanished. But you can't domesticate God says Isaiah the prophet. That was his message, not just to Hebrew exiles, hanging their harps on the willow trees by the banks of the Euphrates, but to the whole of posterity. And in order to hammer the message home he resorted to poetry. How can you domesticate a God who sitteth upon the circle of the earth, who stretcheth out the heavens as a curtain and spreadeth them out as a tent to dwell in.

One of the most moving films I have ever seen was 'A Man for all Seasons'. It is the story of how King Henry VIII made Sir Henry More Lord Chancellor of England, thinking he could manipulate him, in order to accommodate the law to certain domestic ambitions. The King miscalculated. Sir Henry would not be manipulated. Impervious to flattery and every form of psychological pressure, he endured imprisonment, rats gnawing at his flesh, torture and finally execution, without flinching. This saint points beyond himself to the God who was the source of his courage and serenity, the God of all seasons who can't be manipulated.

### 3) *The fact of the Divine image in man*

In modern culture two attitudes towards man stand over against each other in sharp contrast. On the one hand we are bombarded by sounds of optimism. They come to us from the cosmic optimism of Chardin, who despite his awareness of recurring crisis is the arch-apostle of hope. They come to us from Harvey Cox who declares that the forces that cripple and corrupt human freedom have no longer the power to determine man. They come to us even more exuberantly from William Hamilton (the Death of God theologian) who contrasts the melancholy of T. S. Eliot with the man of celebration and rejoicing in the Beatles' film 'A Hard Day's Night'.

On the other hand we come across writers, equally tough minded, who claim that the appropriate mood for our time is that of pessimism. So Malcolm Muggeridge writes 'The curtain, indeed is falling, if it has not already fallen, on all the utopian hopes which have prevailed so strongly for a century or more'. The same sentiment is supported by Rabbi Rubenstein in his very radical book *After Auschwitz*. Rubenstein argues that the incineration of six million Jews in the last war discredits optimism for all time. It reminds us, argues the Rabbi, of the fact of original sin expounded by Augustine and Calvin. Man's inhumanity to man in the twentieth century proves that these two much maligned theologians were bang on target.

The Biblical doctrine of man is a curious amalgam of pessimism and optimism. With brutal frankness the Bible exposes its heroes as men with clay feet. Moses, the master mind behind Israel's deliverance, was also a murderer. David, poet and mystic, was not averse to liquidating amorous rivals. Peter, the Rock on which the Church was built, was at the same time a broken reed inclined to go to pieces in moments of stress. In this Book there is no attempt made to whitewash human nature. It tears the camouflage from the foolish prides and the idolatries of men—of big tyrants who regard themselves as masters of the destiny of other men on the grand scale and of lesser mortals who gloat over cheaper triumphs.

That is one side of the picture. The other is the incredible optimism of the Bible, especially that of the

New Testament. Jesus addressed the lost, fully expecting them to respond. Paul, who never minimized the grim reality of evil, urged Christians to be more than conquerors. The Apostle John, in days of cruel persecution, must have seen the brutal side of human nature, yet we find him writing 'now are ye sons of God and it does not yet appear that ye shall be'.

Quite so, you say, but can we go on believing in the divine image in man in face of all the available evidence? What about men like the Gestapo and individuals like Eichmann? Is it not extremely likely that the divine image in such men was not just defaced but completely blotted out? On this question we must never dogmatize. The mysterious thing about man is that he is a self-transcending being. By the grace of God he has the freedom to change at any instant.

Dr Victor Frankl, the eminent psychiatrist, who miraculously survived Auschwitz camp, cites the case of Dr J. whom he regarded as a mephistophelean figure. This doctor was nicknamed 'the mass murderer of Steinhof'. He was dedicated to the ghoulish task of sending all mentally disturbed people to the gas chamber. Dr J. was taken prisoner by the Russians, but next morning the door of his cell was open and he was never seen again. It was assumed that with a number of other notorious Nazis he had escaped to South America. Years afterwards Frankl was treating an Austrian diplomat repatriated from the famous Ljublejanka prison in Moscow. This diplomat told him that Dr J. had been in the same prison and had died at the age of forty from cancer of the bladder. During his imprisonment he had behaved like a saint, tireless and selfless, using all his skill and every scrap of his energy to comfort others. How can we dare to predict the behaviour of men?

So in these tough days what we need above all is not condemnation but comfort, not religion as a sedative, anaesthetizing our sensibilities, or as a tranquillizing drug, rocking us to sleep in face of injustices that shout to high heaven, but comfort, as assurance, the knowledge that 'there is something not ourselves that makes for righteousness', the conviction that the God revealed in Jesus is sovereign Lord of History transcending all our efforts to possess him, inseparable from the human nature bearing his own image. 'Comfort ye, comfort ye my people, saith your God.'

# 8) The Rich Young Ruler

*'What lack I yet?'*    Matthew 19:20

It is customary to talk of 'The rich young ruler', but the title is a composite one. 'Rich' is taken from Mark, 'young' from Matthew, and 'ruler' from Luke. The incident must have made a deep impression on those who witnessed it, for the three Evangelists record it. Though there are slight discrepancies in the different accounts, the core of the story in each of the three gospels is essentially the same. They tell of an exemplary young man who wanted to throw his lot in with the new faith and was actively discouraged. Incidentally the whole episode teaches us a great deal, not only about the character of the rich young ruler, but about the character of Jesus as well.

For one thing the episode reminds us of the range of Christ's appeal. Even in the New Testament it is clear that Jesus appealed to a wide variety of people. The common people heard him gladly, so did publicans and sinners, social outcasts like Mary Magdalene, and despised tax-collectors like Matthew and Zaccheus. But they by no means exhausted the list of those upon whom he cast his spell. Nicodemus, a ruler of the Jews—a man of culture and refinement—came to consult him under cover of night. A Roman centurion with an inherent respect for authority was instinctively drawn to him. And the young aristocrat of our text was more than interested—he wanted to become a disciple.

In the second century, Celsus, the first professional critic of Christianity, thought he had damned it once and for all by claiming that the new religion concerned itself with the riff-raff of society. The answer it that it most certainly did, but its range was wider than Celsus was prepared to concede. Many centuries later, Nietzsche, the German philosopher, claimed that Christianity was a religion for cowards, that it was obsessed with what he called the effeminate virtues, and opposed to everything that was rugged and virile in life. And Bertrand Russell regarded the Christian faith as the repository of all that is reactionary and life-denying in our society.

This is arrant nonsense. Those who would question Christ's universality are laying themselves wide open to ridicule. From the very beginning he appealed to all sorts and conditions of men. Not only to slaves grovelling in bondage, but to leaders of the intellectual calibre of Paul. Not only to ordinary people, but to geniuses of the stature of St Augustine. Not only to the proletariat, but to men of royal lineage like St Columba and St Thomas Aquinas. Not only to the untutored, but to literary giants like Milton, Tolstoy and Doestoevsky. Not only to the meditative, but to men of action like Edward Wilson and David Livingstone. The range of Christ's appeal is truly uncanny.

For another thing we are reminded of Christ's uncompromising honesty. The rich young ruler was manifestly sincere. Only a man who was deeply moved would have rushed up to Jesus and, without any polite preliminaries, blurted out 'Good master what must I do to inherit Eternal Life?' This man is more than mildly interested, he is captivated by the New Teacher; yet Jesus throws cold water on his enthusiasm and rejects him as a potential disciple.

We would do well to ponder this episode when we grapple with the dilemma of modern evangelism. Any technique whose aim is to rouse the emotions and to bludgeon the intellect into a dumb acquiescence stands mercilessly exposed by Christ's treatment of the rich young ruler. Cheap evangelism with its obsession for counting heads is here categorically condemned.

The rich young ruler's offer of discipleship must have presented Jesus with a difficult decision. Up to now his little band of followers was rather undistinguished and somewhat dishevelled, and this aristocrat would have been a tremendous asset, and would have added lustre to what was looked upon as a disreputable venture. But Jesus sternly suppressed the temptation. He refused to encourage him because he knew that in the end of the day this kind of patronage does the Christian cause more harm than good. How very different from the present-day Church which hails the conversion of an unbelieving philosopher, scientist or popular writer as a momentous event about which God must be frightfully pleased.

Jesus never collected disciples on false terms. Never once did he claim that Christianity solved all our problems. On the contrary he made it plain that there is a sense in which Faith in God increases our tensions and creates new challenges—'Blessed are ye when men shall revile you and persecute you and shall say all manner of evil against you falsely for my sake'. And we who are dedicated to the task of Christianizing our world must emulate the Master's honesty. We must tell people that Christianity, far from making life more easy, in fact makes it more difficult.

Furthermore this episode remains us of Christ's capacity to induce a sense of need. What an extraordinary thing when you come to think of it. Here is a village carpenter, an itinerant preacher, someone who socially does not count; and over against him is an aristocrat—a member of an *élite* class, possessing all the privileges and advantages people so inordinately value, yet he seeks Jesus out and humbly addresses him as Master. In the presence of Jesus, the rich young ruler was conscious of his own inadequacy.

We can reasonably assume that this particular encounter was not a first meeting. More than once this would-be disciple had listened to Jesus expounding the gospel of the Kingdom of God. And as he listened he found himself saying, This man has something which I lack'. The effect was cumulative, at last reaching a crescendo which made him cry, 'What must I do to inherit Eternal Life?'

Need is not a sign of man's weakness, but a badge of his greatness in the scale of existence. Man needs more than bread and the satisfaction of physical wants; he needs music and art and literature. He needs more than aeroplanes to traverse the skies and telescopes to scan the distant stars, he needs vision, without which the people perish, and values to help him live at peace with himself and others.

Need comes to different people in different ways. To one man it comes out of a sense of failure. When he has betrayed his ideals, lost his integrity and acquiesced in evil, he can no longer deceive himself. No doubt psycho-therapy can help by unearthing hidden motives and dispelling morbid fears, but it cannot induce in any man 'the peace of God that passeth all understanding'.

To another man need comes out of a desire to trace a thread of meaning through the labyrinth we call life. So it came to Tolstoy. A count, born and bred in privilege, a rich landowner, a novelist with a universal reputation, outwardly he appeared to lack nothing, but inwardly he was tormented by a sense of sheer blank meaninglessness of things. This is what in the end drove him to God.

Still to another man need comes out of a deep sense of his own inadequacy. Like the righ young ruler of the gospels, his conduct may appear exemplary and he may have kept all the commandments, but nevertheless he is aware of dreams, aspirations, beckoning possibilities standing over against him, mocking him by their dizzy unattainable heights. So it came to Abraham Lincoln. When his responsibilities were light, God was no more than an interesting speculation, but when as President of the United States he had to take momentous decisions, God became his refuge and his strength.

This then is the crux of the problem, how to create in people a sense of need. Modern man is so self-sufficient and so self-satisfied that he does not feel strongly inclined to bow the knee and call himself a miserable sinner. If we preach sin along the traditional lines, the only response we get is a sophisticated and supercilious smirk. There is only one course left open to Christians—the lifting of Christ up in the fulness of his cosmic New Testament stature—the lifting of Christ up in the arena of economics, politics, education—the lifting of Christ up in the arena of our individual dilemmas, till like the rich young ruler we are compelled to cry, 'What must I do to inherit eternal life?'

Still the stubborn question remains. Why did Jesus discourage the rich young ruler? Listen to his conditions—'Go and sell that thou hast and give to the poor, and come and follow me'. No wonder this solution has continued to disturb the succeeding generations. If the absolute renunciation of wealth is the precondition of salvation, we are, I am afraid, all lost. It is pointless to divide people into two categories, those with money and those without it, for the simple reason that in our kind of society we are all dependent on the accumulated wealth of others. We are all involved in what Thomas Carlyle calls 'The cash nexus', and there is no escape.

How then are we to interpret the injunction Jesus gives to the rich young ruler? It is clear that it is not a universal rule imposed upon all Christians, but a particular prescription dealing with a rather unique case. This aristocrat of the gospels was transparently sincere. Not only was he a pillar of moral rectitude, but he also possessed an attractive personality. One version of the story says that Jesus looked upon him and loved him. Why then was he rejected as a disciple? This seems to me to be the explanation. In his injunction to sell all that he had, Jesus is in effect saying this. 'You say you want Eternal Life, but do you really know what that means? And if you do really want it, are you prepared to give up your most treasured possessions—your wealth, your comfort, your social prestige —that you may attain it? If you regard Eternal Life as the pearl of great price, you must be ready to renounce all the lesser pearls in exchange.' Jesus, with his uncanny insight into human nature, knew that for the rich young ruler discipleship, however desirable, was secondary. The God which claimed his basic loyalty was money, and the social prestige which went with it.

It is not enough to be interested in religion. Anyone can be, for, contrary to popular opinion, it is a fascinating subject. Nor is it enough to be enthusiastic about religion the way we can be about sport and stamp-collecting and politics. Nor is it enough to be good and sincere and attractive. Like the rich young ruler we may possess all these qualities and still fail to pass the test Jesus applies to all Christians. The story of the rich young ruler drives home one point and one point only—the totalitarian nature of Christian discipleship. Jesus did not enjoin us to cultivate a moderate and well-balanced interest in religion. He enjoined us to love the Lord our God with all our hearts, with all our minds and with all our strength. He expected the kind of discipleship that was all dominating, dwarfing all other interests by its intensity.

In a way this is the theme of Somerset Maugham's novel, *The Razor's Edge*. Larry, the hero of the book, belonged to the social *élite* of Chicago. Comfortably off, popular, compellingly handsome, he was engaged to a girl of his own class. But Larry was also profoundly interested in religion, and he knew God would never become real to him till he became the master passion of his life. So, to the surprise of his friends, and the consternation of his family, he broke off the engagement, threw up a lucrative business and surrendered himself totally to the quest of finding God. And he got his reward. He came to experience what the Bible and the mystics and men of spiritual discernment throughout all ages mean by Eternal Life.

# 9) A Study of Judas

John 13

JUDAS, the most tragic figure in the Bible, is also the most pathetic personality in all history. Other classic names like Hamlet, King Lear, and Faust pale into insignificance before him. What an unrivalled opportunity he had and how stupidly he bungled it all. Under cover of night he led the Sanhedrin to the Master's hiding place, and was therefore as guilty of Christ's death as if he had actually wielded the hammer that drove in the nails.

Judas is such a dark enigma and has exercised such a spell over the human imagination that twenty centuries after his death men are still trying to explain him. Only recently the novelist, Eric Linklater, wrote a book about him, and the questions he poses are the ones which have been asked from the beginning. What prompted Judas to engineer Jesus' downfall? What were the mixed and complex motives that inspired the callous betrayal? What precisely were the stakes in his programme of calculated duplicity? Let us briefly in passing consider a few of the classic theories that have been advanced.

There is the view that Judas was only a puppet, pulled by invisible strings. The scheme of Christian salvation, the unfolding of the Divine purpose in history, and the fact of the Cross demanded a villain. Judas was the man chosen. Driven by forces which lay beyond his own volition, he was predestined by God to act in the drama of the crucifixion which was ordained from the foundation of the world. Christians must strongly repudiate such a view, not merely because it completely exonerates Judas, but also for the more serious reason that it plays sheer havoc with the character of the God Jesus revealed to us. A God who could, cold-bloodedly as it were, contrive such a situation bears no resemblance at all to the Father of our Lord Jesus Christ.

There is another view which asserts that Judas was mercenary-minded, and was consequently motivated by greed. In his role as treasurer, he thought he could negotiate a deal with the Sanhedrin, so he bargained to betray Jesus for thirty pieces of silver. But this theory, once we examine it, is even more untenable. The Sanhedrin were determined to do away with Jesus, and were prepared to pay any price to arrest Him without causing a public commotion. Judas, a shrewd bargainer, if he had so wished could have extracted far more than thirty pieces of silver from Caiaphas, the High Priest. Whatever motive prompted his action, we can safely discount that of greed.

Most famous of all, there is the theory sponsored and popularized by De Quincey. His argument runs something like this—Judas, far from being a bad man, was in fact a misguided saint. Certain that Jesus was the long-promised Messiah, the Holy One come to ransom and redeem his people, he staged this mock betrayal in Jerusalem in order to force Christ's hand. What Judas really wanted was to make Jesus come out into the open, to proclaim the rule of God, and demonstrate his own Kingship once and for all. When this plan miscarried, Judas was so mortified that in a fit of remorse and disillusionment he committed suicide. There are some writers, including one or two of our most notable preachers, who lend support to this view. I am suspicious of this claim, not merely because it grossly over-simplifies a very complex question, but even more so because it runs counter to the New Testament attitude in no uncertain manner. To white-wash Judas of all guilt may sound attractive, but unfortunately such a naïve romanticism does not do justice to the facts.

These theories, if we took them seriously, would reduce the drama of the crucifixion to a pious but essentially pointless farce. At best it could only amount to a piece of play-acting, an insult to our intelligence and an outrage to our spiritual sensibilities. The truth is that Judas was a tragic figure on a grand scale. He was not a devil incarnate as so many are inclined to believe, nor was he utterly and totally depraved. This is tragedy of such cosmic proportions that it would have reduced even a Shakespeare to silence. It takes the New Testament with its stark unadorned portrayal of the facts, and its strong sense of Divine Drama, to do justice to it.

In his gospel, John, with sparing economy of language, describes a scene which heightens for us the tragic atmosphere surrounding the Cross. In the Upper Room, where the first Lord's Supper is enacted, Jesus makes one last bid to save Judas from himself. Before supper the Master washed the disciples' feet, and during supper he gave him the sop which was a symbol of honour. But Judas spurned every friendly overture. The iron had entered his soul. Then came his departure from the inner circle of the disciples. Walking away from the supper table, he left the room for ever. This is how scripture, with masterly succinctness, puts it: 'He went immediately out and it was night.' Yes night without, and a deeper, darker night within. In turning his back on Jesus, Judas was pitting his strength against God, and defying the moral constitution of the universe. The tragedy of Judas reminds us of—

### 1) *Our superficial understanding of human nature*

There is a stubborn belief shared by Communism and Democracy, that human nature is a pliable substance, which, provided it is subjected to the right pressures, responds accordingly. The sponsors of this creed would have us believe that if a man is placed in the proper physical environment, and his mind is exposed to correct ideas, he will as a reasonable and intelligent being conform to a civilized pattern of behaviour. Hence, an inordinate emphasis on environment and education as the necessary conditioning factors. Judas plays absolute havoc with such a facile theory. He juts out in the midst of history to remind us that despite the best education and the most ideal environment, there is something brutally unresponsive and frighteningly demonic in human nature.

Can we think of anyone who had a better chance then Judas Iscariot? What an environment! A prominent member of the inner nucleus from which the Christian Church sprang—a man who was for three full exhilarating years in daily touch with none other than the Son of God himself. Could anyone wish for a more congenial climate? And what an education—the sermon on the mount, the parables with all their range

74

and depth, the piercing insights and revolutionary ideas of the Master himself. Yet it all proved fruitless. Judas, the arch-traitor, behaved as if he had never been in contact with the purest personality of all times.

There is a basic irrationality in human nature which has not the slightest regard for our neat man-made regulations, and confounds our most confident predictions. On a smaller scale we have all come across our Judases. We have known men and women who had every chance—a good education, the most promising environment imaginable, the best of parents, yet deliberately they have betrayed their inheritance and sunk to the lowest depths of moral degredation. The Cross rebukes our sentimental *naïveté* regarding human nature. It reminds us that man is capable of preferring a Barabbas to a Jesus, of choosing the worst and crucifying the best.

## 2) *In the second place the tragedy of Judas reminds us of the inadequacy of human idealism*

Judas, it would appear, was a zealot, a fervent nationalist and a political firebrand. He and his fellow-conspirators were dominated by one ambition—to see the yoke of Rome smached and Israel restored to her former position of proud independence. This we can readily understand, for nationalism is by no means dead. We have witnessed its recrudescence in our own time all over the world, and its devotees are prepared to go to any length to achieve their desired ends. This is the reason Judas hailed the coming of Jesus with such unqualified enthusiasm. To him the Messiah was invincible. Not only would He break the power of foreign domination, but at the same time He would usher in the promised revolution. So, ironically, Judas, the greatest idealist among the twelve, has become known to us as the traitor of traitors.

Perhaps we should not be unduly surprised. History bears witness to the fact that the most shocking crimes against humanity have been perpetrated not by creedless sceptics, but by flaming idealists. There is nothing more destructive in this life than the man who is tethered to the wrong ideal. No doubt both Napoleon and Hitler were perfectly sincere in pursuing their dreams of a unified Europe, but in the process they inflicted untold misery on millions of their fellow-men. Whatever is wrong with Communism, no one can accuse it of lacking a passionate ideal. Whether it is the right one is a question on which the fate of the world hinges.

The tragedy of Judas is the tragedy that bedevils every misguided idealist. His aim is either to improve himself or humanity, and bring into being a new social order, but somewhere along the line things get hopelessly tangled and mixed up. He finds that there is an unresponsive core at the heart of life he had not reckoned with, and that, in order to achieve his ends, he is forced to use means which mock the ideal he began with. The most dangerous enemy of Christianity in the world to-day is not a coarse-grained materialism, but the passionate idealism that is divorced from Jesus Christ.

3) *The tragedy of Judas reminds us of the inner meaning of the Christian Faith*

There is a sense in which Judas was a man of faith. Not only did he believe in God, but he also believed that his own nation was specially favoured—as the

76

vehicle of an invincible Divine purpose. He was also a
rigid dogmatist. To him the long-promised Messiah
was a political conqueror or nothing else. His mind
was closed to any other conceivable interpretation, and
when Jesus refused to conform to the traditional Jewish
conception of Messiahship, Judas rebelled and tried to
force his hand.

At Caesarea Philippi, and no doubt more often in
private discussion, Jesus had assured his anxious disciples that death could not defeat his purpose, that the
Cross on which he was destined to die was but the
prelude to the Resurrection. If Judas had only exercised
a little patience. If only he had waited a few more
days. If only he had been present in the Upper Room
when Peter, beyond himself, burst in and announced
the stupendous news, 'The tomb is empty, the Lord is
risen', and Cleopas, having run seven miles from the
village of Emmaus, followed close behind crying, 'We
have seen the Master, and recognized him in the breaking of bread'. It is the Resurrection which makes the
betrayal of Judas so unbearably tragic. In short, Judas'
fatal sin was his failure to trust Jesus.

In varying degrees we all share this fault with Judas.
We are perfectly prepared to believe in God, provided
things are going well; or even at the worst, provided he
supplies us with a proof that he will win in the end.
But it is this mentality which Jesus castigates in the
New Testament—'an evil and adulterous generation
seeketh after a sign and there shall be no sign given
them'. It is precisely this demonstrable kind of proof
which God refuses to supply. So we find ourselves bang
up against the inescapable question—what do we mean
by faith?

Faith, like a strong reliable rope is made up of more

than one strand. Classical theology mentions three which intertwined round one another constitute the meaning of faith. One strand is known by the Latin word 'notitia' which means understanding. The second strand is called 'assensus', adequately translated by the word assent. The third strand is 'fiducia', and this is best translated by the word 'trust'. Now it is clear that in every act of faith these three strands are present. If I say, 'I believe in God', there is a sense in which I have an understanding of God, however dim, and in which I give my assent, however weak it may be, but the real meaning and marrow of the Christian faith is neither understanding nor assent, but trust.

This is the New Testament emphasis and it finds unequivocal expression in Paul. Luther in his famous doctrine of justification by faith is saying the same thing in different words. Professor Emil Brunner is interpreting both Paul and Luther when he writes: 'Faith is not primarily faith in a truth, not even in the truth that Jesus is the Son of God, but is primarily trust in this Lord and Redeemer Himself.' And the Shorter Catechism puts it superbly as usual. To the question, 'What is faith in Jesus Christ?' it answers: 'A saving grace whereby we receive and rest upon Him alone for our salvation, as He is offered to us in the gospel.'

The Christian is not called upon to solve all the dark enigmas and baffling mysteries of life. These are enough to drive him not to faith, but to despair. But he is called upon to trust Jesus Christ, to place his reliance in him, persuaded that he is King of Kings and Lord of Lords. Jesus declared that God is our Father and that we can proceed on the understanding that his strong everlasting arms are underneath us.

And this is the question, 'Do we trust Him?' Are we prepared to accept his word and say:

> Here in the maddening maze of things
> When tossed by storm and flood,
> To one fixed ground my spirit clings;
> I know that God is good!

# 10)  Jesus and the Children

*'Unless you turn round and become like children, you will never enter into the kingdom of Heaven.'*          Matthew 18:1–14 (NEB)

THERE are only two incidents in the Gospels which involve children. There is the one which is so often read at Baptisms which tells how the disciples tried to keep children away from Jesus, how furious he was and how he insisted in taking them up in his arms and blessing them. And there is this one which tells how Jesus took a child and held him up as the model Christian. Without the passport of a childlike nature, it is not possible to enter the kingdom of heaven.

There are no stories in the whole range of the Gospels which speak more eloquently of the humanity of Jesus. We are all suspicious of the man who has no time for children. Cruelty to children evokes an immediate angry response anywhere in the world. In our prisons the murderers of children are held in special contempt —so much so that sometimes they have to be protected by the prison authorities.

While we are eternally grateful that the Gospel writers included these two incidents, nevertheless the passage concerned has been responsible for more slop and syrup than anything else in the whole of the New Testament. There is the gentle Jesus, meek and mild, of our sentimental hymns, embracing children, that bear not the slightest resemblance to the obstreperous little monsters that have so often driven teachers, baby-sitters and parents to a state of spluttering impotence.

Now this sentimentality is bad enough in itself, but it is doubly bad in that it affects our ideas of how Christians should conduct themselves in the world. In both stories it is significant that Jesus holds up children as the model citizens of his kingdom. In reading chapter 18 we notice that at first 'little ones' refers quite clearly to children, but later—the transition is almost imperceptible—'little ones' refers not to actual children but to potential disciples. So if you and I start with sentimental ideas of children, we're bound to end up with equally sentimental notions of what the Christian faith really is.

What then was Jesus saying to us in these two incidents? Is this it? Look at how innocent and guileless children are. Emulate them and a passport into the kingdom of heaven is automatically yours. That kind of talk smacks more of Rousseau than of Christ. Rousseau and all the apostles of Romanticism proclaimed the gospel of the essential goodness of man. According to this view the child enters the world in innocence. The spark of the divine which he brings with him is only gradually extinguished by contact with what has been described rather preciously as this 'naughty world'. You recall how Wordsworth puts it:

> *Not in entire forgetfulness,*
> *And not in utter nakedness,*
> *But trailing clouds of glory do we come*
> *From God, who is our home.*

In view of this doctrine of man, it is not surprising

that the Romantic Idealists of the nineteenth century arrived at some astonishing conclusions. They implored us to get rid of the priest and the magistrate, and all they stood for. Leave man alone, they said. Drag him out of the shades of the prison house we call religion. Set him free from all political entanglements. Allow him to develop to the full his natural goodness and Utopia, if not round the corner, is definitely round the next one. But such ideas could not last. They were pitted against a grim reality that has a habit of riding roughshod over all our naïve sentimentalities. And it wasn't the Christian Church that exposed and ridiculed this romantic myth. The person who did it more effectively than anyone else was Sigmund Freud, the eminent doctor and psychologist. Working in Vienna among cultured people, brought up in ideal surroundings, he uncovered in men and women all sorts of disturbing and destructive forces, which operated even before they were born. It would be quite wrong to tie Freud and the Bible up in one tidy bundle but it would be true to say that, in his celebrated clinic in Vienna, Freud discovered something which the Bible knew and had affirmed a long long time before, that man is 'conceived in sin and born in iniquity'.

When Jesus took a child and said 'unless you turn round and become like children ye shall not enter into the Kingdom of heaven' he was not asking us to emulate their so-called innocence. What then are the special qualities children possess which make them model Christians—the sort of qualities adults too must acquire if they are to qualify for a passport into the kingdom of God?

We have claimed that it isn't their guilelessness. Is

it their dependence then? Of all God's creatures the child is the most helpless. From the moment he utters his first cry in an alien world he is utterly dependent on others for warmth, for food and above all for love. So on the basis of this indisputable fact, it is tempting to argue that just as children are completely dependent on their parents so we can do nothing of ourselves. Face to face with the contingencies and challenges of life we must cast our burden entirely upon God.

It is precisely because there is an important element of truth in this contention that it is such a dangerous attitude. There is a kind of pietistic other-worldly religion which emphasizes our nakedness, our emptiness and our poverty before God. The argument goes something like this. Science and the dazzling achievements of technology haven't added anything to the sum total of human happiness. On the contrary they have paved the way to universal frustration and mass neurosis. So with varying degrees of refinement and crudity we go on to say 'Man of himself is lost and helpless'. His salvation consists in acknowledging his own utter bankruptcy and his total dependence on God.

I feel convinced that this attitude is a misreading of the basic message of Christianity. Bonhoeffer, that doughty warrior, who slew so many mythological dragons, exploded this myth of a childish dependence on God, with his detonating phrase 'man come of age'. What precisely did Bonhoeffer mean by the famous four-word phrase that has caused more consternation in theological and Church circles than perhaps any other utterance of this century?

I still don't know for certain what Bonhoeffer meant by that cryptic remark, but I think I know what he did not mean by it. He did not mean that man had abandoned his evil ways and had effected what the Biologists call a mutation. He did not mean that man had suddenly put his adolescence behind him and had miraculously attained to a new level of maturity. Bonhoeffer was no fool. He knew his world better than most of us. He was under no illusions as to man's capacity for evil and sadistic wickedness. He did not live in a fool's paradise. He was in fact hanged by the Gestapo. What then did he mean by his celebrated phrase 'man come of age'?

He meant, I think, that we can no longer indulge in a childish dependence on Divine intervention to extricate us from dilemmas of our own making. The *'Deus ex machina'*—the God outside the machine—who intervenes now and again to remove the spanner from the works, is no longer credible, says Bonhoeffer. God does not bestow His benediction on the abdication of intelligence and moral responsibility. Prayer is no substitute for hard work. Isn't this what Augustine meant by his famous dictum, 'laborare est orare'—to work is to pray.

At St Andrew's University I knew a student who spurned Augustine's wise counsel, and substituted prayer for hard work. Never away from his church and its incessant demands he neglected his studies. On the eve of the final degree exam he put his trust in a *'Deus ex machina'*—the God who intervenes—but when the list of passes was put up in the quadrangle his name did not appear.

And take it from me no *'Deus ex machina'*, no busybody cosmic manipulator will miraculously get us out of the desperate messes of our own making. Our world is riddled with rank injustices. Righteousness demands more than pious prayer—it demands intelligent legislation and social responsibility. Racialism will not be abolished by a fiat of the divine will, but by an open acceptance of our basic common humanity. The model Christian is not a man who wallows in a bogus sense of dependence, he is a man who under God is prepared to act in an adult responsible manner.

But Jesus held a child up as the model citizen of the kingdom of God. If I am right in arguing that the thing about children that impressed Jesus most was not their innocence, or their dependence upon adults, what precisely was the quality that attracted him? What innate characteristic of the child made him say 'except ye turn round and become like children ye shall never enter the kingdom of God'? I maintain it was their openness—the quality which children everywhere in the world possess in super-abundance.

Children are open to ideas. They are not prisoners of the closed mind, of the unexamined prejudice, of the built-in dogmatisms, which not even God himself can dislodge. This is what Anne Sullivan, the teacher, discovered about Helen Keller, the blind spoilt little girl who tyrannized her parents. She was a little savage who ate her food like an animal and flew into tantrums at the least provocation. But blind and deaf though she was her mind was open to ideas. That was her salvation.

This is a desperate need today—openness of mind. Without it there is no hope of survival. Why did Jesus weep over Jerusalem crying 'Oh Jerusalem, Jerusalem, that killest the prophets, and stonest those that I have sent unto thee, how often would I have gathered thy children . . . and ye would not'. Was he a clairvoyant who foresaw the destruction of Jerusalem by the Romans in AD 70? I think not. He was crying for all prisoners of the closed mind, for all the Luddites and Canutes and reactionaries of history, who, resisting change, pit themselves against the inexorable judgements of God.

What is the number one sin in the Protestant Church to-day but that of the 'closed mind'. We have sanctified our parochialisms. We have absolutized our smelly little orthodoxies. We have invested our denominations with a dimension of ultimacy and we are not prepared to admit we may be mistaken. Few of us are as frank as the Duke of Wellington who is alleged to have barked at his officers in staccato fashion, 'God knows I have many faults, but being wrong is not one of them'. If this Protestant Church of ours is to survive the seismic upheavals of history, our minds must be open to far-reaching radical changes. We must be open to the secular challenge. We must be prepared to listen to thinkers like Bonhoeffer, Harvey Cox, Langden Gilkey and Gregor Smith who tell us that to-day Christians are called on to witness to God not within the Church but in the world. We must become immersed in its culture, its education, its urban upheavals, its politics, in all its significant happenings. We must stop talking of the role of the laity. Elders are not ecclesiastical flunkeys, celestial postmen, distributing communion cards so many times a year. They have to become theologians, relating their belief in God with what is actually happening in the world. The Church must be declericalized and the revolutionary doctrine of the Priesthood of all believers must be rediscovered. On the lintel of every Church in the land the words should be engraved 'change or perish'. God has already engraved the message with a pen of iron on the pages of history.

Again, children are open to persons. The Pharisees hated Jesus because his scorching realism was a threat to their bogus security. Children on the other hand loved him because instinctively they knew he was an authentic person. According to Professor Gordon Allport, the American psychologist, children at an early age are absolutely free of the snobbishness and of the social and racial discriminations which characterize adult society. This is so till about the age of eleven.

We could argue without any trace of hyperbole that our survival as a society and indeed as the human race depends on cultivating an openness one to another, on the acceptance of mutual toleration. America has learned this lesson the hard way, and, though the crisis is by no means solved, she is at least facing in the right direction. South Africa and Rhodesia will suffer before they learn. On this most important of all issues Christians should have been blazing crusaders, stabbing the slumbering conscience of the world awake, before the secularists shamed us to it. Modern science has annihilated distance—the earth has shrunk in size. Ours is an electronic age, says McLuhan, and our world is a global village. True, but this conquest of space has only exacerbated our problems. The number one threat to the survival of our race is not the hydrogen bomb, but proximity without community. Physically we live cheek by jowl, but psychologically we are poles apart. The Jews and Arabs geographically are on top of one another, but ideologically what a distance separates them!

The best treatment of the race question I have so

far read is by the American dramatist Arthur Miller. It is in his one and only novel called *Focus*. The hero is a man called Simpson; of genuine Anglo-Saxon pedigree. He could trace all his forebears back to England, Scotland or Ireland. But he looked uncommonly like a Jew, especially in the region of the nose. In the white suburb of New York where he lived, Jews were not in favour. When he tried to join a golf club he failed. Once or twice he tried to put up at classy hotels and found they were always full. A gang of youthful thugs that hated Jews began to persecute him. To begin with it was fairly trivial—breaking the milk bottle at his door, upsetting his dustbin—but gradually it became more serious—threats on the telephone, stones through his windows, physical assaults when out for a walk. His protestations as to his Anglo-Saxon pedigree fell on deaf ears. One night a neighbouring Jewish shopkeeper, by the name of Finkelstein, was viciously attacked by the gang. Simpson felt compelled to go to his assistance and in so doing got a bit of a battering. Later he walked to the police station and reported the assault. The sergeant at the desk picked up a pad and began writing. Looking up he said to Simpson, 'You are a Jew too aren't you?' And Simpson answered 'Yes'. In the interval between question and answer Simpson had a stunning revelation that instantaneously dissolved all his structures of prejudice. Being human—that was the important thing—not being Jewish or American or Anglo-Saxon. And on the heels of this disclosure a great peace flooded his whole being. Arthur Miller, an agnostic, is an indefatigable preacher of this gospel of openness. For Christians this is the right focus—a child-like openness, not just to our own kith and kin, but towards all the children of men.

One brief final word. Children are open not just to ideas, to other people but also to God. The late Principal John Baillie claimed that as a child he could not remember ever having doubted the existence of God. 'I would as soon', he wrote, 'doubt the existence of my own parents.'

Ah, but John Baillie was born into a remarkably pious home— the Free Church manse of Gairloch in Western Ross. There are millions of children who are born into homes marked either by spiritual neutrality or a truculent this-worldly secularism. If we have any respect for the correct use of language how can we talk of such children being open to God.

I feel fairly certain that we can. It is true, of course, that in their conception of God children are to begin with utterly dependent on their parents and on the conditioning culture in which they are reared. Quite so, but children are not natural atheists. They are not born with a built-in structure of prejudice against the idea of God. They are open to him and at an early age have the ability to embarrass adults with questions showing a profound theological insight.

One of the most attractive things about children is their capacity for trust. And trust significantly is the essence of faith. This is the note that rings out so triumphantly in both the Old Testament and in the New. 'Though he slay me, yet will I trust Him', cried Job. And Jesus, dying in excruciating agony whispered with his last breath, 'Into thy hands I commit my spirit'.

Dietrich Bonhoeffer, to whom I have referred already, was a brilliant theologian—an intellectual with a ruthlessly analytical mind. But above all he was a man with a childlike faith in God the Father of Our Lord Jesus Christ. He was preaching at an evening service in prison camp when the Gestapo came for him. 'Prisoner Bonhoeffer come with us', they shouted. He knew this meant execution. On the way to the door he spoke to one of the worshippers, Lieutenant Best, an English officer, 'If you get back to England carry my regards to Dr Bell, Bishop of Chichester'. And then, without a trace of anxiety on his face, he smiled and said, 'This is the end—for me the beginning of life'.

In the presence of massive evil and personal tragedy we need a faith which is rooted in childlike trust, not in scintillating cleverness. In this post-Einsteinian, post-atomic age, a childish faith deserves all the savage strictures hurled at it by men like Russell, Sartre and Camus. But a childlike faith is different. It cuts its way through all sophistries and subterfuges, and grasps the God who is ultimate Reality, the ground of our existence. Only a childlike faith will enable us to sing with Whittier:

> *I know not where His islands lift*
> *Their fronded palms in air;*
> *I only know I cannot drift*
> *Beyond His love and care.*

# 11) The Meaning of Care

THERE is an ancient parable of care which goes like this. 'Once when "Care" was crossing a river, she saw some clay; she thoughtfully took up a piece and began to shape it. While she was meditating on what she had made Jupiter came by. "Care" asked him to give it spirit, and this he gladly granted. But when she wanted her name to be bestowed upon it, he forbade this, and demanded that it be given his name instead. While "Care" and Jupiter were disputing, Earth arose and desired that her own name be conferred on the creature, since she had furnished it with part of her body. They asked Saturn to be their arbiter, and he made the following decision which seemed a just one: Since you Jupiter, have given it spirit you shall receive that spirit at its death, and since you, Earth, have given it body, you shall receive its body. But since "Care" first shaped this creature, she shall possess it as long as it lives. And because there is now a dispute among you as to its name, let it be called "homo" for it is made out of "humus"—earth.'

This parable makes it clear that the capacity to care is the meaning of being human. The person who lacks the ability to care for others is seriously sick and is a potential danger in the community. Psychologists in dealing with certain kinds of neurotics have found that the chief block impeding recovery is the incapacity of the patient to feel. Some of the patients are brilliant intellectuals who hold down important jobs, but who in the realm of human relationships are no better than living machines that cannot experience genuine feelings.

What we are witnessing is the emergence of apathy as a dominant mood of our day. In March 1964 the *New York Times* reported, 'For more than half an hour thirty-eight respectable law-abiding citizens watched a killer stalk and stab a woman in three separate attacks in Kew Gardens'. When questioned by a journalist, each one said that he did not want to get involved. In April of the same year the *Times* once again came back to the same subject. In an impassioned editorial it referred to a crowd that urged a deranged youth, clinging to a hotel ledge to jump, calling him 'yellow' and 'chicken'. 'Are they any different from the wild-eyed Romans watching and cheering as men and beasts tore each other apart in the Colosseum? Does the attitude of that mob bespeak a way of life for many Americans? If so, the bell tolls for all of us.' And Pamela Johnson reporting the murders on the moors of England writes, 'We may be approaching the state which the psychologists call affectlessness'.

Apathy goes hand in hand with violence. They provoke one another. Where there is lack of passion and enthusiasm indifference grows and the situation becomes explosive. When life is empty and apathy increases, when one cannot affect or genuinely touch another person, violence flares up. It is a demonic demand for contact, a mad urge forcing touch in the most direct way possible. Resenting anonymity the

92

adolescent has forced the group to take notice of him by destructive behaviour. To be actively hated is almost as good as to be actively liked. It breaks down the utterly unbearable hell of anonymity and aloneness.

In such a world, where apathy hand in hand with violence is emerging as a dominant mood, it seems to me that Christians strategically speaking are in a strong position. In his Gifford Lectures Toynbee claims that a big factor in the incredible success of the early Church was its capacity for care. More than the Government or the municipal authorities, says Toynbee, the Christians cared for the needy, the despised and the destitute. This is still our secret weapon and it is sheer blasphemy to talk of evangelizing a world where man is protesting against his anonymity, till we take seriously the charter which is ours. Christianity and care are indivisible and that for various reasons.

For one reason Jesus taught that God cared. Does God care? From time immemorial men have posed this question and they are still asking it. This is not a conundrum conjured up by the theologians but a question that is thrust upon us by the whole of life. The agnostic asks it. So does the ordinary man who has never read any of the classical proofs of the existence of God. So at times does the devout believer, carrying about with him the agony of faith and doubt. Every time we see a war killing and maiming millions of men, a tidal wave crashing in from the ocean wreaking untold havoc, a dear friend die of cancer, we ask this question. Our philosophy of life, our whole system of values, our attitude to the mystery of human existence depends on the answer we are prepared to give.

There are those who argue that the nature of the

universe rules out any possibility of a caring God. It is too vast and impersonal. The receding nebula, the million light years, the immense unfathomable distances mock a belief in a personal God who calls us by name and counts the hairs on our head. In our efforts to cope with life the last thing we can count on is supernatural help.

On the eve of his eighty-third birthday, Bertrand Russell was taken to hospital for a fairly serious operation. In the course of a visit a friend talked about the reality of the life to come. Russell dismissed this as sentimental cant. But, argued his friend, the present world is riddled with all sorts of injustices and inequalities, there must be a redressing of the balance in the shape of immortality. At this point the aged philosopher raised himself on his elbows in bed. His rasping voice was heard reverberating down the hospital corridors, 'The universe is unjust, it does not care a rap for the individual'.

There are others who argue that man's inhumanity to man is the real count against God. When Ivan the Terrible sat upon the throne of Russia he murdered whole families to gratify his whims. In torture he took delight, and in one day consigned to slaughter 15,000 of his own subjects with every species of malignant cruelty. And Ivan is not alone. History has also thrown up its Attilas, its Neros, its Borgias, its Torquemadas, and its Napoleons. We still speak of the divine image in man but Pascal may have been more accurate when he wrote: 'Man is an uncomprehensible monster.' Byron is not more complimentary. He is 'a two-legged reptile, crafty and venomous'. We may comfort ourselves that the enormities of Ivan and his fellow torturers are of ancient date and now impossible. Not so. Think of the millions of peasants Stalin sacrificed to prove a very dubious economic dogma, and the millions of Jews Hitler incinerated in his devotion to a stupid and savage myth.

But Jesus did not live in easy times. He had witnessed mass exterminations and many crucifixions but nevertheless he taught that God cared. He was not the first in history to teach this, but he was the first to make it central. Before he came the belief hovered at the outer edge of life, but Jesus made it the axis round which everything in the universe revolved. Christianity rests on the assumption that God cares. To question it is to undermine the entire structure and cause it to tumble to the dust. If we had one vote to cast for or against, to whom would we give it, Bertrand Russell or Jesus Christ?

Jesus taught that God cared, but he went much further than that, he himself cared, so much so that some twenty centuries after his death we still refer to him as 'the man for others'. What is the most impressive thing about this Jesus who was born into an unbelievably cruel and callous world? Is it his teaching with its piercing paradoxical insights into the mysteries of life? Is it his brilliant epigrams still so apposite and so disconcertingly true? 'To him that hath shall be given and to him that hath not shall be taken away, even that which he hath.' Or is it his personality, standing like a solitary Mount Everest towering above the rest of the human race? All this would mark him out as truly unique, yet what impresses me most about Jesus is none of these things, but the depth of his care for others. Like a volcano this care may remain quiescent for a season, while he expounds a particular truth, demolishes a popular fallacy, engages in cut-and-thrust argument with his enemies, but, ever and anon, it erupts, reminding us that love burns with elemental fierceness at the heart of the Eternal.

His care for men leaps out at us in his teaching. It forms the subject matter of all his greatest parables— the prodigal son, the good Samaritan, the pearl of great price—and, even when he was expounding his parable on the judgement to come, the smouldering volcano of his compassion burst into flame. 'In as much as ye have done it to the least of these my brethren ye have done in unto Me.'

His care for men leaps out at us in his miracles. What prompted Jesus to perform his mighty works while he was here on earth? What was the real motivation behind the healing miracles? There are those who argue that the miracles were proofs of his messiahship. Just as an ambassador presents his credentials at the court of St James, so Jesus presented his works of healing to the world. They were the testimonials of his divinity. I am sure this is the wrong interpretation. Jesus wrought his mighty works, not to draw attention to himself, but because he was implacably opposed to unmerited suffering. He made the lame to walk, the blind to see, the deaf to hear, not to demonstrate super-human powers, but because he passionately cared for men.

His compassion for men leaps out at us from his whole personality. The acid test of human sympathy is not glib pronouncement, but costly participation. Jesus did not merely preach tolerance towards the misfits of society, he consorted with them to the dismay and consternation of the respectable. He did not clamour for sterner measures against criminals, he identified himself with them. This is what the New Testament means when it says, 'He was numbered with the transgressors'. So outrageous was the conduct of Jesus in the eyes of the apostles of law and order that he was branded a criminal, tried as a criminal and finally executed as a criminal. If he had lived under British instead of Roman rule, he would not have been crucified, he would have been hanged by the neck till he was dead. In his total identification with the despised and rejected of men, Jesus was the embodiment of care.

Jesus taught that God cared: Jesus himself cared but that is not the whole story. Jesus empowered men to care for one another. Every year in Spring we celebrate in the Church one of the most important Christian festivals—Pentecost. And how did the first Christians celebrate the coming of the Holy Spirit? They gave away all their money and shared all things in common. In other words their action was an experiment in voluntary communism. Naïve, utopian, stupidly impractical! No doubt; but, however misguided, the first Christians demonstrated to all history that Christianity and care for men are inextricably mixed up.

In his book *Christianity and History* Professor Herbert Butterfield reminded us that, when the Church had the power, she was guilty of every crime in the calendar. This is true, but it is also true that in her best moments the Church remained true to the basic impulse of Pentecost. It was the Church that organized the first hospitals in Europe. It was the Church that brought into being our ancient universities. Who first exposed to the world the inhumanity and the squalor of our prisons? A devout Christian by the name of Elizabeth Fry. Who first moved heaven and earth to free the slaves throughout the length and breadth of the British Empire? Not a humanist or an agnostic but a Christian called William Wilberforce.

Without this imaginative care for the disinherited of the earth all our efforts at evangelism will prove abortive—and deservedly so. By far the most disturbing challenge to the Church to-day is that the secular conscience, at its best, is more insistent and more imperious than that of conventional Christianity. There are millions of Christians who profess Christ as the Lord of all life, yet show no concern for the victims of racial prejudice and economic exploitation. As long as this is so Christians cannot expect to stab the slumbering conscience of our world awake.

Care must express itself not just in intimate inter-personal relationships but also in those of society at large. The decision of the American supreme court to desegregate schools is a good example of this wider interpretation of care. This is what Professor Tillich means when he says that '*agape*'—the Greek word for Christian care—must be demonstrated not just in private morality but in political structures and in imaginative constructive social legislation.

This is illustrated by two eminent Victorians—General Gordon and Lord Shaftesbury. General Gordon was a military genius and at the same time an eccentric Christian saint. Other-worldly to a unique degree, he practically starved himself, and gave his army pension to help war widows beneath the contempt of the War Office, and to educate waifs and strays from the streets. His biographer, Lord Elton, estimated that by this

98

means Gordon touched the lives of not more than four hundred people. Let us not belittle this achievement. How many of us have positively affected four hundred lives?

Lord Shaftesbury, Gordon's contemporary, was also a devout Christian, but he employed a different strategy. Instead of depleting his bank account to care for individuals in dire distress, he wielded the weapon of social legislation. He was the man who in the teeth of massive opposition pushed through the Factory Acts which saved millions of women and children, working in mines, from premature death.

For the Christian to-day the choice is not one between private, unobtrusive acts of individual charity on the one hand, and much publicized enactments of social legislation on the other. It is not an 'either/or' decision but a 'both/and'. The present-day Christian must be a General Gordon and a Lord Shaftesbury rolled into one.

# 12)  Nerve Centres of Protestantism

THERE are those who believe that the outlook for Protestantism is less than encouraging. They base their assessment on the assumption that the spirit of Protestantism in its heyday gave rise to the divisive and disruptive forces that split Christendom down the middle. In view of its past history, it is not likely to create the sense of oneness the world so desperately needs.

The critics claim that Protestantism spawned nationalism with its consequent progeny of disorders. Nor can we deny the truth in this accusation. Luther was intensely nationalistic. He was inclined to associate internationalism with corruption and nationalism with purity. This applied to economics as well as to theology. Reinold Neibuhr argues that Hitler's nationalist socialism was not a historical accident but the demonic consummation of this attitude.

The critics also accuse Protestantism of creating capitalism. This is the thesis propounded by Max Weber and though he may have exaggerated, there is no doubt that Puritanism gave a new drive and dynamism to business. Thrift, foresight, punctuality and perseverance were Protestant virtues. Is it purely accidental that Calvin's Geneva became famous for the manufacture of clocks and watches?

And of course the critics blame Protestantism for the scandal of sectarianism. The autonomy of individual judgement was given pre-eminence over the claims of community and schism was the result. This tendency to split and divide has been described somewhere as the fissiparous fertility which belongs to the very nature of Protestantism. If our generation is moving away from unbridled *laissez-faire* capitalism to responsible collective planning, from schism to unity and from narrow nationalism to world consciousness, communism and humanism are more likely to promote this spirit. So say the denigrators-in-chief of the Protestant faith.

In the struggle for survival there are two main dangers that lurk in the Protestant path. One is that of mere adaptation, a walking of the tight-rope of conscious adjustment in a fluid and rapidly changing society. A certain amount of adjustment is unavoidable but if this is all we have to offer a sick world, poised over the void of no meaning, then we richly deserve the doom which it is not possible to escape.

The other danger is that of slavish imitation. There are trends in present-day Protestantism which are somewhat alien to the prophetic spirit that launched it. These include such innovations as episcopal authority, a creeping sacramentalism, an encroaching of ecclesiastical rites and a more extensive use of symbolism. It is sometimes alleged that the austerity of Protestant architecture and the bleakness of its worship resulted in a starvation of the spirit which cries for more colour, more ritual and more drama in life. This need expresses itself in the absurd jamboree of Odd Fellows, Buffaloes, Masons and kindred fraternities. The introduction of colour might not be a bad thing in itself, as long as it is not a pallid imitation of other traditions. If such imitations have no root in our own tradition, they'll fail to carry conviction and they will be powerless to stem the swirling tide of indifference that seems to engulf us.

Protestantism stands at the cross-roads. The only way it can survive is by demonstrating once again the critical yet creative spirit which enabled the first Reformers to declare war on tyranny and dislodge it in the name of God. Is the Protestant faith a spent force, a thing of the past, a quaint anachronism which once served a useful purpose but is becoming increasingly irrelevant towards the close of the twentieth century? While we must not underestimate the disruptive forces that show not one iota of respect to sacrosanct institutions, nevertheless we believe that what is of the essence of Protestantism belongs to the undying freedom of the human spirit. We live in an age of Protest with God nostalgically remembered but no longer obeyed, with families corroded and cities growing like great tumours, with vast states restless in the grip of political paranoia. It is in such a climate that we, the spiritual descendants of Luther and Calvin, are challenged to a new awareness of the nerve centres of our Protestant heritage.

Consider the nerve centre 'By faith alone'.

This is the battle cry of the Reformation, but there are those who argue that this slick slogan is as false as it is dangerous. For many it means no more than a passive acceptance of a dogma sanctified by the passage of history. Such people are strong on correctness of belief, and by no means so strong on correctness of behaviour. We have all met pillars of Christian orthodoxy who could also be described as ambitious egomaniacs or neurotics in bondage to various kinds of compulsion. Was it this contradiction between creed and conduct in the very early Church, James was rebelling against, when in his celebrated Epistle he rebutted Paul's emphasis on 'faith alone'.

Mowrer, the American psychologist, pours scorn over the classical Protestant doctrine of justification by faith alone. Among other things he accuses it of encouraging laziness, complacency and a facile fatalistic attitude towards our moral imperfections. He makes it absolutely clear that he agres with James rather than Paul. 'Works' are necessary, argues Mowrer, in order to make amends for past misdeeds and in order to build up a trustworthy character. Though he savagely criticizes the traditional Roman Catholic system of penance as trivial, an insult to all who regard themselves as responsible adults, he argues that the idea of penance is a sound one psychologically. He further claims that Protestantism could work out a system of moral exercises which could satisfy man's inner demand for some form of expiation.

I am convinced that Mowrer misunderstands Paul and the Reformers who were the apostle's interpreters. Did this New Testament emphasis encourage any dichotomy between belief and behaviour? Was Paul lazy? Think of his colossal achievements—his missionary journeys—his theological reflection on the meaning of the Christian faith—his martyrdom. Were the great Reformers lazy? Ask Luther and Zwingli and Calvin and John Knox whether the doctrine 'by faith alone' encouraged complacency? Were David Livingstone, Karl Barth and Pastor Niemoller morally indifferent? One and all they have demonstrated the mystery of faith, that it is only when men acknowledge their own moral bankruptcy and impotence that they exhibit the power of God.

This is an intoxicating age, intoxicating in the vastness of its knowledge, its engineering miracles and its utilization of the natural resources of the world. Yet despite all this, and we must on no account despise it, there is one thing we lack—the ability to believe. We analyse, we observe, we classify, we pursue painstaking research. But to believe is something else. It is tempting to hand our religion over to the historian, the psychologist, the sociologist, but what above all we need, as individuals and as a society, is to recover the capacity to believe. It goes without saying that theology, criticism and reflection are important, but the ground of Christian experience is none of these but faith.

Consider further the nerve centre 'The Priesthood of all believers'.

The Reformers reacted against sacerdotalism and their avowed ambition was to give the laity a more responsible place in the life of the Church. This they undoubtedly achieved in Geneva, in Scotland and in Germany but the proposed revolution was not nearly radical enough. After some four centuries of Protestant tradition we still talk of the 'role of the laity in the Church'—a curious use of the English language when we consider that the laity constitute at least about 99 per cent of the Church. The laity, despite the revolutionary doctrine of the Priesthood of all believers, are constantly thought of in negative terms. Would we not be on firmer ground if we were to talk negatively of the role of the clergy who because of their special calling no longer happen to be laity?

The compendium edited by Bishop Stephen Neill

and Hans Rudi Weber entitled *The Layman in History* makes one thing clear beyond all disputing. The expansion of Christianity throughout the centuries owes more to the witness of the laity than to the work of the clergy. In Latin America the evangelical community grew from 12,000 in 1900 to 9,000,000 in 1961. In Brazil, where the population increased three-fold over the last sixty years, the Protestant population has increased thirty-five-fold. This dynamic growth is related to the fact that the new Churches springing up are lay centred.

In their book *God's Frozen People* Mark Gibbs and Ralph Morton draw our attention to four great differences between the Church of the first three centuries and the Church of to-day. The early Church had no ecclesiastical buildings. The apostles never 'went to church'. The Church was the people of God, meeting in someone's house. Nor had the Church any clergy in the modern sense of that word. Neither were there theological colleges, though it is highly probable that ordinary people were theologically more articulate than in any subsequent age. And the life of the Church, so fully secular and lay, had no relation, except one of opposition, to what we now call the 'establishment'. In a strong paragraph they then remark: 'These four things—buildings, clergy, theological colleges and social respectability—are all things we take for granted for the Church. We cannot conceive of the Church without them. What did the early Church do when it did not have to trouble about these things? It converted the Roman Empire.'

It is imperative to declericalize the image of the Church in a secular age. The truth is that political, economic and cultural questions have achieved a level of complexity which precludes direct intervention by the clergy. This fact makes the lay ministry the only viable form of the Church. Laymen, unlike religious professionals, do not have to make Herculean efforts to become involved in the secular. They already stand at the key points where religion and life come to grips with one another. The task of the clergy is to help the laity towards greater theological maturity.

Finally there is the nerve centre we call the prophetic role.

According to popular tradition the prophet is a sort of eccentric seer, possessing occult powers, something equivalent to what in the Highlands of Scotland we call the second sight. This is a crude misunderstanding of the prophetic role. We must on no account equate prophecy and prediction. One or two of the Old Testament prophets may have possessed some capacity for prediction, but that is not what marks them out. It was rather their ability to interpret the events which took place in the world around them. Like delicate seismograph instruments they sensed the far-off tremors of coming earthquakes. They anticipated the shape of things to come and related them meaningfully to the will of God in history.

In his *Protestant Era* Tillich writes:

*The Protestant principle contains the divine and human protest against any absolute claim made for a relative reality, even if this claim is made by a Protestant Church. The Protestant principle is the judge of every religious and cultural reality including the religion and culture which calls itself 'Protestant'. . . . It is the guardian against all the finite and conditioned to usurp the place of the unconditional in thinking and in acting. It is the prophetic judgement against religious pride, ecclesiastical arrogance and secular self sufficiency.*

The Reformation motto was 'Ecclesia reformata sed semper reformanda' (the Church reformed, but always to be reformed). The notion that the Reformation is complete or even that it can ever be completed, is a denial of what 'reformation' in the Protestant sense really means. There is not much point in the Church fighting secular idolatries such as white supremacy and the deification of sex when she succumbs to idolatries in the shape of rigid ecclesiastical structures. 'We must', said Niebuhr, 'fight the falsehood in our truth.' As the Old Testament prophets reminded Israel, so we must say to the Protestant Church, 'you are not exempt from the judgement of the living God'. This must be said unambiguously, disconcertingly and disturbingly.

The Protestant principle, while not despising tradition, is orientated towards the future. This strategy is not easy to define but it has its own authority and integrity. It means that we can trust God without question, but that we may put a question mark over against every human account of God. It means that we are absolutely committed but that all statements about the exact nature of that commitment are tentative. It means that our faith is rooted in ultimate security, not in any immediate security. The Protestant venture involves a risk, but it is a risk taken within the context of a promise, a placing of our trust in God but not in man.